KOREAN STUDIES DISSERTATION SERIES NO. 7

Reflective Language Teaching in the Korean Context

Kil Su Park

Jimoondang
Seoul, Edison N.J.

Jimoondang (President: Lim Samgyu)
514-7 Munbal-ri, Gyoha-eup, Paju-si, Gyeonggi-do, 413-756, Korea
Phone: 82-2-743-0227 E-mail: edit@jimoon.co.kr
82-2-743-3192~3 E-mail: sale@jimoon.co.kr
F a x : 82-2-743-3097, 82-2-742-4657
Homepage: www.jimoon.co.kr
ISBN 978-89-6297-006-7

The National Library of Korea Cataloging-in-Publication (CIP)
Reflective Language Teaching in the Korean Context /
Kil Su Park
Paju: Jimoondang, 2009 (Korean Studies Dissertation Series; No. 7)
Includes bibliographical references and index
ISBN 978-89-6297-006-7 93740 740.7-KDC4 420.7-DDC21 CIP2009000106

Printed in Korea

Preface

English language teaching in foreign language contexts is complex work. Among the many variables including the teacher, students, curriculum and methodology, the methodology factor is especially important since it usually stipulates the roles of the others. So, a lopsided emphasis on one specific area in methodology results in an unintended negligence of the other areas. Over the past decades, both the research and the national curricula of Korean English language teaching and learning have heavily depended on the theory of Communicative Language Teaching (CLT). Without doubt, CLT is a robust language teaching method. In Korean ELT contexts, however, the full implementation of CLT has to encounter many practical difficulties.

The major difficulty is that the students do not much perceive the need to communicate in the target language. Therefore, teaching English as communication is a task all but impossible in classroom situations. In the English classrooms in Korean grade schools, teaching the target language as communication is often incompatible with teaching it to enhance the grammatical competence. According to Pachler and Field (1997), teaching grammar for better understanding of the linguistic system should be acceptable in foreign language teaching as long as it is helpful to the learners.

The CLT approach, however, has persistently prevented teachers from directly teaching grammar even if it is teachable or learnable. Its proponents believe that teaching discrete points of grammar will surely fall short of a meaningful exercise. Since the CLT methodology presupposes the learners' intention to communicate, meaningfulness is considered as the most important among many characteristics of CLT. But the reality is that the students rarely want to speak the target language for communication in the foreign language classroom. In this situation, the use of CLT for developing communicative competence among learners is to be abandoned, and the battle for implementation cannot but be an uphill one.

There are also other problems that impede the implementation of CLT. Firstly, the teachers have to confront the students who may have two ironically opposing traits. On the one hand, they are postmodern kids whose epistemes are drastically different from those of older generations. On the other, due to the inveterate societal influence of Confucian ideas, they still view teachers as knowledge holders and if the teachers do not display their knowledge in lectures, the students get greatly disappointed. The CLT-oriented teachers who like to use communicative games will not do very well in such a classroom. Moreover, the traditionally bent learners have low tolerance of ambiguity and high inhibition coming from peer pressure. They usually keep silent in the classroom even when they are called by name.

Secondly, another possible impediment for CLT is too much assigned curricular content to finish in a limited time. For the teachers there is always not enough time to cover the assigned portion. To make matters worse, they have to make the reluctant learners to be engaged in some form of communicative activity of which the students soon get bored unless the teacher pours a lot of effort into planning and staging it.

Thirdly, teachers feel the constant pressure from the school administrators, from parents, and from the society in general. They all demand a fast result and a visible outcome. Education thus has a tendency to degenerate into a manufacturing labor where only the product matters and the process of teaching and hence the quality of teaching are hardly a concern of any magnitude.

The last and perhaps the most influential factor that hinders a successful implementation of communicative language teaching and learning is the excessive examination competition. As in Japan's case (Gorsuch, 2000; Namoto et al., 2000; Okano & Tsuchiya, 1999), in the past it may have been the driving force of success since it has motivated a large proportion of young people to achieve and to believe that they can compete for the society-appointed prizes. Because everyone is in the game, however, the competition becomes intense, and because everyone is deemed capable of achieving, "there are no alibis for failure" (Green, 2000, p. 422). This is a cruel game but at the same time it is an inevitable concomitant of meritocracy. In relation to education, however, the problem is that the competition makes the national household spend an exorbitant amount of private budget in learning English. An extreme view is that the richer you get the better opportunities to learn English you can afford to give your children. The sad reality is that Korean students are so dissatisfied with the English teaching at schools that many bring home private tutors or take courses in private language institutes to learn English. This extracurricular learning is imposing a heavy burden on the budget of each household. The fact is that, according to Shin (2001), the money spent for English teaching in Korea amounts to approximately 8 billion dollars annually as of 2001. Now the total amount is expected to double by 2009.

A more basic, fundamental problem with the CLT approach

is that it is a method that had never been proved or tested in our educational environment when it was introduced. So, in a sense, everything was experimental. If we piece together what has happened in many of the English classrooms so far, CLT seems like an incompatible software with our societal system because there are so many clash elements. CLT in its original form is a solution that was designed to fit into the post-industrial system of the Western countries whereas ours is still a system for the mass-production of intellectuals and technicians, a so-called knowledge-factory system of the industrial society, as exemplified well in the highly preferred standardized examination systems at every societal level. We may be making vain efforts to apply the CLT model to a "different" system like ours. So there must be a phenomenon of overload which could make the whole system down.

In this situation what can we possibly do in order to solve the perceived problem? Is there any solution at all? First of all, we need to find some debugging gimmick to solve this problem of incompatibility. The solution to be proposed in this study is the method of Reflective Language Teaching (RLT). It is a method of English language teaching in view of "reflective teaching." In brief, "reflective teaching" is a self-help method that involves the teacher's ability to make rational choices and to assume responsibility for those choices (Ben-Peretz, 2001; Borko et al., 1997; Emery, 1996; Ferguson, 1989; Henderson, 1989; Richards & Lockhart, 1994; Roberts, 1998; Roth, 1989; Schön, 1983; Shulman, 1987; Smyth, 1989; Tom, 1997; Wallace, 1991). With this ancient but revisited pedagogical methodology, teachers will be able to regain confidence, empowered to endeavor their spirit of "continuity of learning" (Bell & Gilbert, 1996, p. 6). By the help of this method, they will also be able to develop the long-desired professional competency in their teaching life (Jeong, 1999; Kim, 1999; Lee, 1999; Lee, 2000).

To make a long story short, this book based on my doctoral study is by and large about Korean education; it is especially meant for an alternative solution seeker looking for the possible "third way" awaiting somewhere out there and delving into the problems and the efforts to address the emerged problems of, say, improved English education in Korea. The basic assumption is that educationwise, as in other aspects of national life, Korea seems to have achieved greatly as the world now acknowledges and at the same time troubled herself for long with the problem of sustainability upon the paths to catch up with the global educational powerhouses far ahead of her. Amidst these undertakings, amidst the trials and errors, and amidst the hopes and despairs is a highly trained but still not fully functioning "language force."

So the big question is, how will we as an English educator in Korea address this problem of long-brewn inefficiency or somewhat dubiously defined or contended efficiency so as to gain the so-called competitive edge? And this is the very question that this book is poised to provide an answer for as well as offering a place for contemplation or for "reflection," although the author is well aware of the challenges being daunting.

Acknowledgements

First of all, I thank my Lord for bestowing upon me enough strength and all that I needed to do this study and get it published. I then wish to extend sincere appreciation to my academic advisor, Prof. Cha, Kyung-whan, for his constant help throughout my study at Chung-Ang University. A special debt of gratitude must also go to Prof. Lee, Jae-young, Prof. Kim, Hae-yeon, Prof. Ku, Hee-san, and Prof. Lee, Wan-gi for being my reviewers and for all the friendly encouragements lavished.

My sincere thanks are due to the teachers who willingly participated in the survey, especially to Mr. Park, Cha-ryang who teaches at Kyeonggi High School, to Ms. Kang, Eun-mi who teaches at Onyang Girls' Middle School, and to my brother who teaches at a High School at Muju. I also deeply appreciate the help of the undergraduate and graduate students at Chung-Ang University who gladly lent themselves to the survey. Without their generosity, this book would not have been possible.

My heartfelt thanks are due to my folks at home, including my brothers and their family, for their affection and prayer. My gratitude must also go to my wife and my daughter who have been watching me all the while with concerned looks. Finally, gratitude is also extended to the Jimoondang staff for all their supports and professional assistance and especially to Lim Sam-gyu the president for agreeing to publish this book.

K. S. P.

Contents

Index of Charts

Index of Figures

Index of Tables

I. INTRODUCTION

1.1 Background of the Study

The seemingly well-established prestige of Communicative Language Teaching (CLT)[1] is now being challenged. The brunt of the attack comes from American foreign language educators who insist that learning a language *for* communication is different from learning a language *as* communication and that the primary aim of foreign language teaching be to enhance the "learners' semiotic system" that to a certain extent involves teaching grammar (Pachler & Field, 1997, p. 54). Although one correct definition of the CLT approach is hard to provide because of its widespread scope and influence in English Language Teaching (ELT) today, a possible consensus is that English, either as a second or foreign language, should be taught in order to develop learners' communicative competence and that the most effective teaching, therefore, lies in teaching

[1] The term is used as a synonym of Communicative Approach (CA) in some literature, although the latter is usually thought of as having a much broader denotation. For a brief historical summary or recent proponents and developers, see Brown, 2000, pp. 266-267; Knight, 2001, in Candlin & Mercer (Eds.), pp. 147-166; and Park, 1987, pp. 14-18.

it *for* communication and *as* communication. In this regard we should say that the CLT approach presupposes the learners' intention to communicate. However, according to Pachler & Field (1997), the students don't much perceive the need to communicate in the target language, even in the U. S. secondary-school foreign language classrooms.

In the school environment where the instilling of need for communication is hardly attainable for one or more practical reasons, the very purpose of CLT for developing communicative competence among the learners is stranded, and the efforts for implementation cannot but be an uphill battle[2]. In a number of reports in the literature that deals with CLT innovations in EFL contexts, the voices of complaint and doubt are paramount. Wu (2001) reports that teachers and teacher educators in China found it difficult to use CLT. He cites a 5-year longitudinal case study undertaken by Wang (1999) at East China Teachers' University, which tested the communicative method against the analytical. According to Wu, the experimental classes used the communicatively oriented course book developed by Li Xiaoju while the control group used

---

[2] Even the dauntless Chinese educators are confessing that it is no easy task to adopt the CLT approach in China since it inevitably involves transforming the traditional grammar-translation method. As Xiao (1998) points out, "the inefficient grammar-translation approach is continually reinforced. When some of the students who have been taught with the grammar-translation method turn out to be English teachers, they are most likely to use the same method in their teaching" (Cited in Wu, 2001, p. 197). Little wonder Wu (2001) concludes that "to fundamentally change the situation, teachers must undergo training that will promote their theoretical awareness as well as their linguistic abilities" (Ibid.). In their study of Japanese EFL education, Namoto et al. (2000) also wrote out a similar diagnosis and prescription that the Revised National Curriculum making heavy mention of communication is barely in the works, since the new statement divorces the lofty ideal from reality so that teachers may simply continue to accomodate it to their current modes of teaching. According to Gorsuch (2000), the current mode of teaching is geared to the preparation of national college entrance examination which has to be heavily dependent on the Grammar-Translation Method called *yakudoku* and the Audio-Lingual Method (p. 691).

textbooks whose approach was considered traditional and analytical. The results of this study showed that both the experimental and the analytical classes have strengths and weaknesses (Wu, 2001, p. 196), which means that in some province of China the CLT methodology is either wrongly implemented or not that effective.

Gorsuch (2000) points out that Japanese EFL teachers who have been asked to implement the communicative ethos of the 1992 *Course of* Study framed by the Ministry of Education remain virtually unchanged in terms of their attitudes and beliefs and thus, to a number of Japanese EFL educators' surprise, only a slight change in their actual teaching has resulted (p. 678). Li (1998) also cites several cases of CLT implementation in Asia, most of which are no better than that of China and of Japan. For instance, a study conducted in Vietnam identified class size, grammar-based examinations, and lack of exposure to authentic language as constraints on using CLT. In another case, learners' resistance to introducing innovative CLT methodology was identified in a Pakistan English classroom. Even in Singapore and the Philippines, the long-established grammar-based English language syllabus made the local implementation of CLT challenging (p. 680).

To be as conducive as possible to the felt need in Korean society that schools prepare the coming generations for the unlimited global-level competition and the upcoming English-dominated "Global Village" situations, the Ministry of Education and Human Resources of Korea has placed English learning and teaching high on its agenda. Thus, in 1997, the Development Committee of the 7th Curriculum hustled out a new curriculum for English which was to guide Korean grade school English teaching from the year 2001 onward. As in the 6th Curriculum, the developers of the 7th English Curriculum championed the basic premises of the CLT approach, such as learner-centeredness and meaning-based language learning, as opposed to those of the Grammar-Translation Method or of the Audio-Lingual Method, and based their rationale on constructivism as opposed to the objective, behavioristic principles of learning. Roughly saying, the new Curriculum could be defined as more learner-oriented and more flexible to apply for the teachers, compared to the 6th Curriculum. Without doubt, the spirit of Communicative Language Teaching permeates well in the new Curriculum. One might safely say, therefore, that CLT has achieved a solid basis in Korean ELT, at least on its design level.

It is not difficult at all to see, however, that using CLT on its implementation level at local schools or in each individual teacher's classroom is a different story. To say the least, CLT is yielding a mixed result. Lee et al. (2001), for example, investigate the lasting effects of elementary English education on middle school English education. Their findings net both positive and negative effects: students' interest in English has been increased while their ability in grammar and writing has been lowered. On the other hand, though she finds out discrepancies in terms of theory and practice and of beliefs and implementation, Choi (2000) comes up with an optimistic mood that CLT has bright future (p. 27). The reason for optimism is that English teachers' awareness level is high. And the one condition prescribed for turning the whole stream around is English teachers' level of spoken English. The underlying assumption is of course that if only the teachers acquire the necessary proficiency in English they will do a great job in their classroom.

Among the Korean EFL educators today, as is shown in the above assumption, there exists a persistent, if not potentially harmful, myth that the more fluently one is able to speak English the better English teacher he or she will turn out to be. Basically, English teaching consists of two components, that is, the skills in the target language and pedagogy. The problem is, only the former is unfairly emphasized while the latter is taken for granted. One of the main drawbacks of the theory that underpins the CLT approach is that its main tenet comes from a radically new conceptualization of the nature of language which was "seen as a system for the expression of meaning" (Nunan, 1999, p. 9). This embryonic theoretical limitation seems to have contributed to CLT's lopsided emphasis on the importance of teachers' mastering the target language. There is a catch here, however, in that even if a person knows the target language exceedingly well and speaks it very fluently the feat doesn't necessarily ensure that he or she will be a good teacher. For, if you come along this logic, all and only the native speakers will be able to become good enough language teachers. As far as foreign language teaching is concerned, having a good command of the target language is one thing and teaching it adequately is quite another matter.

Theoreticians often like to talk about pendulum swings (Handy, 1994; Henderson, 1989) and there is also a problem of priority together with the danger of dichotomy. During the 1970s and the next couple of decades, with the new conceptualization of language learning as and for communication on the horizon, the pendulum swing of language education apparently went to the language side but now, due to its propensity, it is deemed to make a slow come back to the other side, i.e., pedagogical side. Of course, as Cochran-Smith (2000) warns us, among the devices of classification, dichotomy has its share of potential danger that may lead us to the path of oversimplification (p. 85). But if we, Korean educators, have to make a decision and make a choice with all this perceived danger, the pedagogical side, not the linguistic side, should be the first and foremost consideration of our educators given the deadlock phase other Asian countries are facing up to in implementing the doctrine of CLT. The change of the direction of the pendulum swing, either by effort or by nature, seems to be the only breakthrough we can expect to make happen as for now.

The problem of EFL education in Japan and other Asian countries is that the reform always came down from the above. Hence results the top-down manner of reform with input being mainly generated by high-level bureaucrats and university consultants. Hardly ever has a bottom-up approach been tried out. So the voices of the on-site classroom teachers are only dimly heard. At the heart of the classroom, however, is the teacher. He or she is standing alone within the four walls, most of the time isolated from outside helps. Students are usually reluctant helpers. The arena called classroom could well be either his or her grave or prison, metaphorically saying. For, only two rules govern the hidden tension of classroom life: unless the teacher establishes control there will be no learning whatsoever, and, if the teacher does not control the students, the students will control the teacher. This is a universal law of classroom teaching regardless of the levels the students are in and regardless of the subjects that are supposed to be taught. Sometimes the power battle overburdens the teacher as in Ahn's (2000) case. In an essay titled "The Reason I Gave Up Teaching," she recollects her job in the elementary school classroom, first addressing the kids: "You guys have been doing fine? Maybe not." Then she continues:

> The school in February is like a 5-day country fair nearing

> the shutdown. With only a few customers left and with the pathetic old songs sounding loud, an ever-growing weariness of that outskirt's Paldo Folk Fair is exactly filled with the mood of a group of public officials ushered for some meaningless political rally. . . . This is how I felt from years ago, even if it's not in February, our school's atmosphere has already taken after that of a café. Kids say whatever they want to say, doing whatever they want to do, and when the teachers of different subjects come before them, they think of them just as a DJ changing music for them with a handful of selections. If the piece is their type of music, they will hear but, if not, fat chance! (p. 36) (Author's translation)

Teaching is a complex job that only looks easy. And teachers are there in the classroom confronting the postmodern kids whose epistemes are made up of such bizarre things as cyber-chatting, comic books, 24-hour video games, amusement parks, ski resorts, bungee jump, luxury shopping malls, brand-name items, jazz dance lesson, Outback dinner, Kentucky fried chicken, grapefruit, blue jean, pro-sports, hip-hop and rap music, the weird ways of using jargons and the intentional disregard of grammar in speech and word coinage, *ad infinitum*. Moreover, to do a successful job, teachers ought to consider a lot of variables other than the learners: the curriculum, the method of teaching, the school and the public, ethical codes, from the macro point-of-view (Barrow & Woods, 1988; Brubacher, 1969); lesson plan, subject matter, effective use of time, classroom management, interactive practice, grouping, audio-visuals and multimedia, assessment, from the micro point-of-view (Freiberg & Driscoll, 2000; Orlich et al., 1998; Van Lier, 1996). Small wonder the technology of teaching is anything but certain, and teachers must learn to live with a lot of uncertainty as an essential component of their professional practice (Henderson, 1989; Kahne & Westheimer, 2000; Labaree, 2000; Yost et al., 2000; Zeichner & Liston, 1987).

There is yet another problem for an English language teacher to deal with: the problem of ZPD (Zone of Proximal Development) and scaffolding. A concept originating from the development psychology of Russian constructivist Lev Vygotsky (1896-1934), ZPD implies "a range of tasks that a child cannot yet do alone but can accomplish when assisted by a more skilled partner" (Eggen & Kauchak, 2001, p. 56). The zone represents a learning situation in which knowledgeable partners or teachers can promote development. It may be noteworthy that the idea is very similar to that of Krashen & Terrell's (1983) "comprehensible input." Bruner's (1983) related notion of scaffolding is based on the social interaction between mothers and very young children. In his own words, scaffolding is defined as "a process of 'setting up' the situation to make the child's entry easy and successful and then gradually pulling back and handling the role to the child as he becomes skilled enough to manage it" (Ibid., p. 60). According to Van Lier (1996), this notion of scaffolding gives us an idea of the dynamism of working within the ZPD as characterized by such features as: 1) the principle of *continuity*; 2) the principle of *contextual support*; 3) the principle of *intersubjectivity*; 4) the *contingency* principle; 5) the *handover* principle; and 6) the *flow* principle (p. 195).

The application of scaffolding to classroom work may concentrate either on one-on-one interactions between a teacher and a student or on small-group activities or on handling the whole class together which often proves tougher due to the usual size of the classroom as in our country. Pedagogical scaffolding is thus a multi-layered teaching strategy, and it allows and/or forces the teacher to keep in mind, at all times, a long-term sense of direction and continuity, a local plan of action, and a moment-to-moment interactional decision-making. Therefore, the multifaceted job of a teacher constitutes a feeder, a nurser, a planner, an improviser, and a decision-maker. Thus the job of a language teacher is only half-completed even if he or she is able to present a perfect modeling through the near mastery of the target language. Far more important half of the job is still there, that is, the skillful presentation of language content on one-bit-at-a-time basis. The consideration of eye-level and arms' reach, and a little bit of frivolity and fun will do a far better job than the native-speaker-like modeling.

Indeed, Vygotsky's ZPD is an apt metaphor for the inter-zone, the "no-man's land where language teachers live and work" (Thornbury, 2001, p. 395). Kramsch (1993) describes the potential of the foreign language classroom to provide "a liminal experience that creates a special space and time at the boundaries between two views of the world" (p. 30). Foreign language teachers are border service who are able to give or not give fatal directions to survive in the borderland. Together with danger and risk, they know they ought to convey the sense of excitement involved in crossing boundaries. Teachers occupy a privileged space on the frontier between two languages, and hence on the frontier between two different cultures when they mediate contact. Here in the border area everything is to be dealt with lightly, with no overt seriousness. This feature of English language teaching Thornbury (2001) calls "the unbearable lightness of EFL," although the metaphorical expression is also used to criticize the easy-going attitude of makeshift EFL teachers who are backpackers when they arrive in the country where they will get the job of teaching English.

As a rule of thumb, language teachers' job is enormous.

Accordingly, they need some outside help, but more often than not the help from outside is gratuitous, and arrives almost always as a form of intervention. The teachers are also beset by problems existing inside. As for developing and effectively using teaching materials, for example, language teachers have to reconcile "materials as constrain" with "materials as empowerment"; hence the job is described as "squaring the circle" which means a try to do something almost impossible by Alan Maley (In Tomlinson (Ed.), 1998, p. 279). Thus Hitomi Masuhara calls teachers "an endangered species" (Ibid., p. 246). Notwithstanding all this difficulty of teaching, not only the untutored public but also teachers or teacher educators themselves assume that the profession of teaching is relatively easy. Hence appears the researchers' curricular focus on the student teachers' mastering the target language skills as shown in Shin (2001): "Highly qualified English teachers will win back the public confidence in education, which in turn will reduce the wasteful drainage of the national wealth by over-dependence on English speaking countries" (p. 193). It is undoubtedly a valuable observation for the current situation we are now in, but simply increasing the level of proficiency won't do the job. If we have to see English education far and wide, the primary focus should be on how to develop its pedagogical scaffolding in Korea. The gap between the haves and the have-nots could better be bridged if a teacher whose English proficiency is no superior yet whose care and enthusiasm are overwhelming takes charge of the children from the have-not classes.

In any case, modern foreign language teaching should bring more focus on pedagogy, ZPD, scaffolding, students, classroom, aims, content, school and society rather than on teachers' oral-aural skills, reading ability, writing skills or more specifically the scores of standard proficiency tests like TOEIC. As Pachler

& Field (1997) have pointed out, it is also doubtful that authenticity is an absolute necessity. For, Alan Hornsey (1994) suggests that plausibility might be a more useful guiding principle than authenticity. He goes on to say that for a language teacher there are other conceptive words that demand attention (p. 7). These are: 1) learnability; 2) repeatability; 3) tangibility; 4) usability; and 5) pronounceability. The eagerly sought-for perfect modeling of a teacher could be a waste of resources in language teaching if the more urgent pedagogical skills do not support it concurrently. The knowledge and skills of the language we are supposed to teach and the professional expertise concerning how to bring the subject matter to the particular classroom are like the two wheels of a cart. If one wheel is abnormally bigger than the other, the cart cannot go afar. One more metaphor we may think of regarding the implementation of the CLT approach in Korea is also related to a horse-driven vehicle: language learners are like a cart and teachers are like a horse. In case the teachers lead the students nice and carefully, the buggy will go on smoothly; however, in the situation where the learners lead the teachers, it will have a lot of difficulties since it has put the cart before the horse.

1.2 Purpose of the Study

With the CLT curricula high on its agenda, English language teachers in Korea seem to have a very limited choice in terms of their leeway of picking up a proper methodology. The influence of CLT is much too strong. But some hallmark tenets of CLT—the learner-centered approach, for example—often bring about unnecessary misconceptions and thus the wrong practices with the concept taken in an either/or disjunctive mentality. Teachers are thus either stuck in confusion or choosing an easygoing attitude toward their teaching, saying, "Don't be so pessimistic! Playing it safe is easy." In any case they need an urgent help for their confusion and their inertia. And the help may first come from inside, from themselves.

To perform their work well, English teachers must be able to give honest consideration to what they do. They have to think about their understanding of the curriculum, their lesson plan, their teaching persona, their way of dealing with emotional problems, and some other big or small educational matters that involve the ability to make rational choices and to assume responsibility for those choices.

The purpose of this study is to design a tangible teacher-helping model that will successfully introduce the reflective teaching methodology to Korean EFL educational contexts so as to have an impact on educational reform. Over the last few decades, an array of imported approaches such as Grammar-Translation Method, Audio-Lingual Method, and CLT have dominated the English language education in Korea. Hardly ever has any bottom-up approach been tried or tested. The model of Reflective Language Teaching will help the Korean English teachers set their own standards to choose the most appropriate method for their teaching. It will show the teachers how they can plan and reflect both individually and collectively, and ultimately lead them to have the necessary intellectual, moral, and critical thinking abilities to be an efficient professional.

1.3 Scope of the Study

In this study the author will consider a series of questions: what exactly is reflective thinking, how are Korean EFL teachers supposed to perform this rather new skill, what beliefs and attitudes do they have for the present, in what way and form should a working model be developed for them to do a better job in the classroom, in what ways are they able to best implement the teaching model, and what are the implications of the answers to these questions for teacher education? These questions will be addressed in terms of a theoretical model development and of practical ways to implement the model in our grade school English classrooms.

The overall study will be descriptive and the research design will utilize both qualitative and quantitative methods in order that the study may lead to a qualitative-quantitative continuum, as recommended in Kim (2000) and elsewhere. The main focus will be on establishing the rationale for the proposed model, on securing the identification of local contexts, and on discovering the ideal structural form of the reflective language teaching model, drawing on the theory of reflection developed by Dewey (1916 and 1933) and Schön (1983 and 1987) as well as their followers before examining the specific variables of English Language teaching.

After reviewing the related literature in the second chapter, the researcher will launch a survey analysis in order to provide the rationale for introducing the reflective teaching to English education in Korea. The preservice and inservice teachers sampled are subjected to a questionnaire that the researcher has prepared to assess their beliefs, perceptions, attitudes, and inclinations. First of all, the purport of the survey research will be discussed, and then the demographic features of the subjects and methods of analysis will be presented before examining the survey results that will be presented in four main categories. For data analysis, both descriptive and inferential statistics have been used. The results and findings will be incorporated into the implementation process in the following chapters.

In the fourth chapter, after providing the assumptions of the proposed language teaching, the tripartite cyclic RLT model will be developed and its structural form will be introduced, focusing on the cyclical operation of the three modules: planning, teaching, and reflection. The description of the expanded RLT model which covers the variables of micro- and macro-reflection will be presented before introducing the combinative model where the five phases of RLT finally develop into seven phases that constitute one full cycle. Then, each of the seven phases of the full RLT cycle will be discussed in some detail with specific examples.

The fifth chapter will be concerned with applying the proposed RLT model to Korean educational environment. In the two-way input system, Teaching receives input from Planning and Reflection; thus, to activate the phase of Teaching the two other phases are activated. The ways to activate the Planning Phase are discussed first, in the process of which the RLT syllabus for *Middle School English I* is designed. Next, the problems of how to implement RLT in Korean contexts are addressed. Then, the ways of implementing individual reflection and collective reflection will be compared and discussed, introducing varying options of collaborative reflection. Afterwards, a new empowered vision of teaching English will be presented identifying the features of RLT and testifying the usability of the proposed model. Finally, the implications for teacher education will be discussed.

The last chapter will contain an overview and the summary

of the study along with some concluding remarks.

In sum, this study is an investigation into possibilities of applying the time-tested idea of reflective pedagogy to ELT teacher development. For realistic reasons, however, the survey in the study was not able to include more subjects in terms of numbers, schools and locations. Also, due to some practical difficulties, the RLT model developed in this study has not been given an opportunity for an on-site test yet. Any teacher or researcher will be welcome to testing this model for its practicality and viability in their working field. On-site language teachers will be able to start writing teaching journal or preparing their portfolio as proposed in the RLT model in order to do some action research.

II. THE NATURE OF REFLECTIVE TEACHING

2.1 The Genealogy of Reflective Thinking

Every discourse has its own value judgment, historicity or Weltanschauung. A genealogy is a deconstructive way of seeing a conceptualization as it actually occurs by bleaching the value and deferring the historicity. It is a mode of reading and a philosophical position that one may take when one does not want to adopt a particular point of view. For instance, Jon Roberts sums up and elucidates in his book (1998) three major models of the person and education. They are: 1) behaviorism and the view of person as input-output system; 2) humanistic psychology and the view of person with self-agency; 3) constructivism and the view of person as constructivist. He criticizes all three, putting off his taking position and comes up with a modified constructivist view of person as social being. He finally places himself in the social constructivist's position. Throughout his book he adheres to this position, adopting a broadly social constructivist approach. As will be shown in a short while, reflective thinking or reflection is an ambiguous term. It could mean a number of different things to a number of different people. So there are a number of positions for anyone to choose from if he wants to consider this theme in any depth. But the author supposes it would be better not to take a position yet; instead, he chooses the deferral strategy until the genealogy approach pays off. Reflective thinking is indeed fit to this approach since it traces back to the days as early as Socrates'.

The western philosopher who first recognized the importance of reflective thinking is Plato. In *Meno*, he argues with a disciple through the mouth of Socrates:

Soc. I know, Meno, what you mean; but just see what a tiresome dispute you are introducing. You argue that a man cannot inquire either about that which he knows, or about that which he does not know; for if he knows, he has no need to inquire; and if not, he cannot; for he does not know the very subject about which he is to inquire.

Men. Well, Socrates, and is not the argument sound?

Soc. I think not.

. . . .

Men. Yes, Socrates; but what do you mean by saying that we do not learn, and that what we call learning is only a process of recollection? Can you teach me how this is?

Soc. I told you, Meno, just now that you were a rogue, and now you ask whether I can teach you, when I am saying that there is no teaching, but only recollection; and thus you imagine that you will expose me in a contradiction.

Men. Indeed, Socrates, I protest that I had no such intention. I only asked the question from habit; but if you can prove to me that what you say is true, I wish that you would.

Soc. It will be no easy matter, but I am willing to do my best for you. Suppose that you call one of your numerous attendants, whichever you like, that I may demonstrate on him.

Men. Certainly. Come hither, boy.

Soc. He is Greek, and speaks Greek, does he not?

Men. Yes, indeed; he was born in the house.

Soc. Attend now, and observe whether he learns of me or only remembers (Cahn, 1970, pp. 16-17).

Thus Socrates asks the slave boy of a geometrical puzzle. At first, he seems to know how the area of square figures are decided, but after Socrates adds to his questions his ignorance is unveiled, and then he gets to understand the principle. This is the paradigm case of what has come to be known as Socratic questioning. After finishing the questioning, Socrates turns back to Meno:

Soc. What do you say of him, Meno? Were not all these answers given out of his own head?

Men. Yes, they were all his own.

Soc. And yet, as we were just now saying, he did not know?

Men. True.

Soc. But still he had in him those notions of his—had he not?

Men. Yes.

Soc. Then he who does not know may still have true notions of that which he does not know?

Men. Apparently.

Soc. And at present these notions have just been stirred up in him, as in a dream; but if he were frequently asked the same questions, in different forms, he would know as accurately as anyone at last?

Men. I dare say.

Soc. Without anyone teaching him he will recover his knowledge form himself, if he is merely asked questions?

Men. Yes.

Soc. And this spontaneous recovery of knowledge in him is recollection?

Men. True.

Soc. And this knowledge which he now has must he not either have acquired at some time, or else possessed always?

Men. Yes.

. . . .

Soc. And if the truth of all things always exists in the soul, then the soul is immortal. Wherefore be of good cheer, and try to discover by recollection what you do not now know, or rather what you do not remember.

Men. I feel, somehow, that I like what you are saying.

Soc. And I too like what I am saying. Some things I have said of which I am not altogether confident. But that we shall be better and braver and less helpless if we think that we ought to inquire, than we should have been if we thought that there was no knowing and no duty to seek to know what we do not know;—that is a belief for which I am ready to fight, in word and deed, to the utmost of my power.

Men. There again, Socrates, your words seem to me excellent.

Soc. Then, as we are agreed that a man should inquire about that which he does not know, shall you and I make an effort to inquire together into the nature of virtue (Ibid., pp. 22-23).

Reading this passage makes one think that human knowledge has not changed much since the days of Socrates. The depth and scope of their thought and insight are just alarming. Many modern educational researchers like to refer to "inquiry" method and "inquiry" teaching and learning. Voi-la! Exactly the same topic Socrates is now juggling with. Moreover, he leads Meno to "inquire together." He not only nudges, pokes, and challenges but also feeds, nurtures, and befriends his student. Indeed, he is the greatest teacher of all times. O'Donoghue & Brooker (1996) mention that "Socrates contrasted perceiving of things outside the self with reflection, the discovery of what is within and brought to birth by questioning and that a variety of contemporary educational theorists reflect this position in their work" (p. 101).

Plato goes on to present a fully developed philosophy of education and nurture in *The Republic*, where all the views are a reflection of his epistemological and political views. His denigration of vocational education is also a good example of his dualistic tendency to separate knowledge and practical action that is implicit in his Theory of Forms (Cahn, 1970, p. 6). His disciple Aristotle, however, proposes in *Nicomachean Ethics* that intellectual virtue is acquired by teaching whereas moral virtue is acquired by practice. In his paper, "Some Thoughts Concerning Education," Locke, on the other hand, saw the principle of all virtue lie in "a power of denying ourselves the satisfaction of our own desires, where reason does not authorize them" (Ibid., p. 136). He continues to insist that parents and teachers instill self-discipline from the time the children are very little and that reasoning with children is of much importance. Surprisingly, as if he were a modern behaviorist, he speaks:

> This method of teaching children by a repeated practice, and the same action done over and over again, under the eye

> and direction of the tutor, till they have got the habit of doing it well, and not by relying on rules trusted to their memories; has so many advantages, which way soever we consider it, that I cannot but wonder (if ill customs could be wondered at in any thing) how it could possibly be so much neglected. I shall name one more that come now in my way. By this method we shall see, whether what is required of him be adapted to his capacity, and any way suited to the child's natural genius and constitution: for that too must be considered in a right education. We must not hope wholly to change their original tempers, nor make the gay pensive and grave, nor the melancholy sportive, without spoiling them. God has stamped certain characters upon men's minds, which, like their shapes, may perhaps be a little mended; but can hardly be totally altered and transformed into the contrary (Ibid., pp. 143-144).

Locke's behavioral propensity is, however, attenuated by the need to recognize a student's inborn character. This balanced attitude toward a human being later has a powerful effect on Dewey when he develops his theory of reflection. Another great philosopher who directly influences Dewey is Kant. In his "Thoughts on Education," he points out that animals are trained, but children must be taught to think. Kant also emphasizes the importance of experimentation in education, the advantages of public education, and the fact that "the best way of cultivating the mental faculties is to do ourselves all that we wish to accomplish; for instance, by carrying out into practice the grammatical rule which we have learnt" (Ibid., p. 193).

Plato, Locke, and Kant, all three of these philosophers constitute the three models of teaching that Israel Scheffler (Ibid., pp. 385-396) provides in a form of remarkably succinct and clear explication. He accurately points out the strength and weakness inherent in each of these three models, which could be summarized as follows:

A. The Impression Model

(1) Philosophical Origin: John Locke.

(2) Theory of Learning: Learning involves the input by experience of simple ideas of sensation and reflection, which are clustered, related, generalized, and retained by the mind. Blank at birth, the mind is thus formed by its particular experiences, which it keeps available for its future use. (See Book II, Chapter I, Section 2 of the *Essay Concerning Human Understanding*.)

(3) Theory of Teaching: Teaching should concern itself with exercising the mental powers engaged in receiving and processing incoming ideas, more particularly powers of perception, discrimination, retention, combination, abstraction, and representation. But, more important, teaching needs to strive for the optimum selection and organization of this experimental input. For potentially, the teacher has enormous power; by controlling the input of sensory units, he can, to a large degree, shape the mind.

(4) Strength: This model sets forth the appeal to experience as a general tool of criticism to be employed in the examination of all claims and doctrines, and it demands that they square with it. Surely such a demand is legitimate, for knowledge rests on experience in some way or other. Further, the mind is, in a clear sense, a function of its particular experiences, and it is capable of increased growth with experience. The richness and variety of the child's experiences are thus important considerations in the process of educational planning.

(5) Weakness: With close affinities to contemporary behaviorism, this model fails to make adequate room for radical innovation by the learner. Teachers do not feed into the learner's mind all that they hold he will have as an end result of their teaching. For, there is a fundamental gap which teaching cannot bridge simply by expansion or reorganization of the curriculum input. This gap sets theoretical limits to the power and control of the teacher; it is where his control ends that his hopes for education begin.

B. The Insight Model

(1) Philosophical Origin: Plato and St. Augustine

(2) Theory of Learning: As Augustine argues in his dialogue, "The Teacher," there is a paradox in learning. The teacher is commonly thought to convey knowledge by his use of language. But new knowledge is not conveyed simply by words sounding in the ear. Words are mere noises unless they signify realities present in some way to the mind. Hence, if the student already knows the realities the teacher teaches him nothing new whereas, if the student does not know these realities, the teacher's words can have no meaning for him. Augustine concludes that language must have a function wholly distinct from that of the signification of realities; it is used to prompt people in certain ways. The teacher's words, in particular, prompt the student to search for realities not already known by him. Finding these realities, which are illuminated for him by internal vision, he acquires new knowledge for himself, though indirectly as a result of the teacher's prompting activity.

(3) Theory of Teaching: The primary function of the teacher's

employing language is not to impress his statements on the student's mind for later reproduction but to become instrumental to the student's own insight. Knowledge is a matter of vision, and vision cannot be dissected into sensory or verbal units that can be conveyed from one person to another. It can, at most, be stimulated or prompted by what the teacher does. It is vision, or insight into meaning, that makes the crucial difference between simply storing and reproducing learned sentences and understanding their basis and application.

(4) Strength: The insight model is strong where the impression model is weakest. While the latter, in its concern with the conversation of knowledge, fails to do justice to innovation, the former addresses the problem of new knowledge resulting from teaching. Where the latter stresses atomic manipulable bits at the expense of understanding, the former stresses primarily the acquisition of insight. In a sense, the former seems to be deeply related to the modern constructivism and to the theory of communicative approach to language teaching.

(5) Weakness: Augustine's paradox of teaching can be simply rejected on the ground that we can understand statements before becoming acquainted with their signified realities. If follows that the teacher can indeed inform the student of new facts by means of language. Thus we are back to the impression model, with the teacher using language not to prompt the student to inner vision, but simply to inform him of new facts. Furthermore, habits of proper execution are not necessitated by the insight model. Insight also fails to cover the concept of character and the related notions of attitude and disposition. In sum, the shortcoming of this model lies in the fact that it provides no role for the concept of principles, and the associated concept of reasons.

C. The Rule Model

(1) Philosophical Origin: Kant

(2) Theory of Learning: For Kant, the primary philosophical emphasis is on reason, and reason is always a matter of abiding by general rules or principles. In thus binding ourselves to a set of principles, we act freely and with dignity. A rational man is one who is consistent in thought and in action, and rationality is an essential aspect of human dignity and the rational goal of humanity is to construct a society in which such dignity shall flower. The job of education is to develop character, that is, principled thought and action, in which the dignity of man is manifest. This model can be differentiated from the previous models in that, while those models are narrowly cognitive, the rule model embraces conduct as well as cognition.

(3) Theory of Teaching: Teaching should be geared not simply to the transfer of information nor even to the development of insight, but to the inculcation of principled judgment and conduct, the building of autonomous and rational character which underlies the enterprises of science, morality and culture. Rational character and critical judgment grow only through increased participation in adult experience and criticism, through treatment which respects the dignity of learner as well as teacher. There must be a gap which cannot be closed by the teacher's efforts alone. He thus must rely on the spirit of rational dialogue and critical reflection for the development of character. In this respect, Kant has a great influence on Dewey in his development of reflective thinking.

(4) Strength: Adoption of the rule model does not necessarily exclude what is important in the other two models; in fact, it can be construed as supplementing their legitimate emphasis. For, intermediate between the public treasury of accumulated

lore mirrored by the impression model, and the personal and intuitive grasp of the student mirrored by the insight model, it places general principles of rational judgment capable of linking them.

(5) Weakness: There is something too formal and abstract in the rule model. And rationality embodied in the relatively young tradition of science is, consequently, judgment which accords with such principles as crystallized at the time in question. To teach rationality in science is to introduce a student to the live and evolving tradition of natural science. To teach rationality in history, however, is also to introduce the student to a live tradition of historical scholarship which is subject to an analogous interpretation beyond the formal demands of reason.

All these three models of teaching influence Dewey's work so much so that he has been criticized as an eclectic philosopher with no original thought. However, it is evident that he is one of the greatest philosopher of education and that he has been a tremendous help for shaping the American education over the past century. Cahn (1970) lavishes his laudation on Dewey, saying that he is the only thinker who has constructed a philosophy of education comparable in scope and depth to that of Plato (p. 201). Roberts (1998) mentions that Dewey's ideas have influenced schooling and professional education throughout the twentieth century (p. 47).

Dewey's philosophy rests on his belief in democracy and the power of scientific inquiry. And his educational theory is widely understood as 'pragmatism,' 'progressive education,' 'children-centered education,' 'new education' or 'democratic education.' However, his main focus is on "good habits of thinking" as clearly shown in the following passage:

> Processes of instruction are unified in the degree in which they center in the production of good habits of thinking. While we may speak, without error, of the method of thought, the important thing is that thinking is the method of an educative experience. The essentials of method are therefore identical with the essentials of reflection. They are first that the pupil have a genuine situation of experience—that there be a continuous activity in which he is interested for its own sake; secondly, that a genuine problem develop within this situation as a stimulus to thought; third, that he possess the information and make the observations needed to deal with it; fourth, that suggested solutions occur to him which he shall be responsible for developing in an orderly way; fifth, that he have opportunity and occasion to test his ideas by application, to make their meaning clear and to discover for himself their validity (Democracy and Education, p. 126).

Reflective thinking that was born in Socratic questioning receives the highlighted focus here. Dewey's idea of regarding thinking as method is continuously emphasized as he further develops his view of reflection:

> To say that thinking occurs with reference to situations which are still going on, and incomplete, is to say that thinking occurs when things are uncertain or doubtful or problematic. Only what is finished, completed, is wholly assured. Where there is reflection there is suspense. The object of thinking is to help reach a conclusion, to project a possible termination on the basis of what is already given. Certain other facts about thinking accompany this feature. Since the situation in which thinking occurs is a doubtful one, thinking is a process of inquiry, of looking into things, of investigating. Acquiring is always secondary, and instrumental to the act of inquiring. It

> is seeking, a quest, for something that is not at hand. We sometimes talk as if "original research" were a peculiar prerogative of scientists or at least of advanced students. But all thinking is research, and all research is native, original, with him who carries it on, even if everybody else in the world already is sure of what he is still looking for (Ibid., p. 114).

Here reflection is viewed as synonymous with 'inquiry,' 'looking into things,' and 'investigating.' This line of thought, in turn, gets to influence the conception building of the following generation of theorists. Also, it is interesting to notice that for Dewey every research is original and valuable. It may provide a clue for Dewey's recognition of the significance of a bottom-up approach to important educational decision-making.

In Archambault (Ed.) (1964), Dewey further defines the characteristics of reflective thinking as follows:

> When we say a person is *thoughtful*, we mean something more than that he merely indulge in thoughts. To be really thoughtful is to be logical. . . . They weigh, ponder, deliberate. . . . They don't take observations at their face value. . . . The word "reason" is connected etymologically with the word "ratio." The underlying idea here is exactness of relationship. . . . All reflective thinking is a process of detecting relations; the terms just used indicate that *good* thinking is not contested with finding "any old kind" of relation but searches until a relation is found that is as accurately defined as conditions permit. In summary, the "psychological" is not opposed to the "logical." As far as an actual process of thought is truly reflective, it is alert, careful, thorough, definite, and accurate, pursuing an orderly course. In short, it is then logical (p. 247).

In addition, he underlines the importance of distinguishing

reflective action from routine action. Reflective action entails the active, persistent, and careful consideration of any belief or supposed form of knowledge in light of the grounds that support it and the consequences to which it leads. Routine action is, on the contrary, guided primarily by tradition, external authority, and circumstance. Therefore, he emphasizes that a person who wishes to be a reflective thinker should have three qualities: open-mindedness, responsibility, and wholeheartedness.

Dewey also argues that reflective thought occurs when the smooth progress of our normal activity is interrupted by perplexity or surprise. He refers to this as a "forked road" situation, in which we are presented with a dilemma which proposes alternative solutions. Once reflection is triggered by some discrepancy or surprise, a complete reflective solution cycle can follow to address the problem. His description could be roughly outlined as follows:

(1) There is a feeling of discrepancy or difficulty likely to be experienced as an emotional disturbance.
(2) We observe to define the difficulty. The more deliberately and critically this is done, the better the eventual resolution will be.
(3) We cultivate a variety of alternative suggestions to solve the problem.
(4) We think through each suggestion and then select the best idea.
(5) We observe again to confirm our theory and adopt it as personal knowledge.

For Dewey, reflection contributes to personal growth because it frees us from a single view of a situation which would restrict how we define problems and so the resulting solutions. Reflection enables us to reframe problems in a variety of ways which therefore allows a wider range of possible solutions, and contributes to change in our perspectives.

An M.I.T. social scientist and consultant Donald Schön's works (1983 and 1987) provide an important recapitulation of Dewey's reflective thinking and has been very influential among the educational society to date. In the face of widespread demands for technocratic ways of operating, he argues that a deep-seated "crisis of confidence" as distinct from "competence" amounts to a manifest inability of the professions to deliver solutions on the pressing environmental, economic, and social problems of our times. According to Smyth (1989), his claims on the "crisis of confidence" are rooted in the argument that those who argue that professional practice should have a demonstrated scientific basis and should adhere to prescriptions deriving from large-scale, objective, outsider-initiated research are ignoring the trustworthiness and relevance of practitioner-derived knowledge (p. 2). Schön (1983) criticizes the academic society in the Preface with the following diction:

> Many people use the term "academic" in its pejorative sense. On the other hand, complaints about the elitism or obscurantism of the universities tend to be associated with a mystique of practical competence. When people use terms such as "art" and "intuition," they usually intend to terminate discussion rather than to open up inquiry. It is as though the practitioner says to his academic colleague, "While I do not accept your view of knowledge, I cannot describe my own." Sometimes, indeed, the practitioner appears to say, "My kind of knowledge is indescribable," or even, "I will not attempt to describe it lest I paralyze myself." These attitudes have contributed to a widening rift between the universities and the professions,

research and practice, thought and action. (Ibid., pp. vii-viii)

Schön's goal is of course to combine the two opposing factors, that is, research and practice, and thought and action. So the outcome is a fine analysis of the distinctive structure of reflection-in-action of five major professions including engineering, architecture, management, psychotherapy, and town planning. Education is only sporadically focused, but he promises to treat the subject more fully in a later book and he did.

The best professionals, as Schön stresses, know more than they can put into words. To meet the challenge of their work, they rely less on formulas learned in school than on the kind of improvisation learned in practice. This largely unexamined process of skilled professionals is the subject of his book which is thought to be provocatively original yet along Deweyan and hence western rationalist tradition. And he confronts both a positivist view and a technicist view of professional expertise. The following passage on two kinds of practitioners eloquently conveys this mood:

> Many practitioners, locked into a view of themselves as technical experts, find nothing in the world of practice to occasion reflection. They have become too skillful at techniques of selective inattention, junk categories, and situational control, techniques which they use to preserve the constancy of their knowledge-in-practice. For them, uncertainty is a threat; its admission is a sign of weakness. Others, more inclined toward and adept at reflection-in-action, nevertheless feel profoundly uneasy because they cannot say what they know how to do, cannot justify its quality or rigor (Ibid., p. 69).

He goes on to say, "For these reasons, the study of reflection-in-action is critically important." By and large, Schön's (1987) notion of reflection encompasses three different modes of reflection: reflection for action; reflection in action; and reflection on action. They are developmental in nature. According to Roberts (1998), this view of reflection is consistent with Dewey's description except that Schön identifies reflection-in-action as the essence of expertise, and therefore as the desirable goal of professional education (p. 51).

So far we have examined a genealogy of reflective thinking in a chronological way. Nonetheless, it appears that this simple linear observation of reflective thinking has revealed an important characteristic of reflective thinking: the origin of this idea is very old and its philosophical implication is quite far-reaching. Now that it is about time to take any position, the author thinks that both Deweyan and Schönian ideas of reflection are most appropriate for the study's future discussion. It is, therefore, no articulation of affiliation toward the three models of education outlined by Roberts or toward the interpretational models suggested by Scheffler. As Dewey made his choice about a century ago, the position to be taken will be inclined to being somewhat eclectic, and as Schön stresses, a bottom-up approach to the professional knowledge will thus be any practitioner's heart's desire.

After all, what is reflection? Dewey's (1933) definition of reflection is "an active, persistent, and careful consideration of any belief or supposed form of knowledge in light of the grounds supporting it and future conclusions to which it tends (p. 6). At a general level, reflection can be defined as "a way of thinking about educative matters that involves the ability to make rational choices and to assume responsibility for those choices" (Ross, 1989; Zeichner & Liston, 1987). Shulman

(1987) highlights the importance of teachers possessing a knowledge base since he believes that, without an adequate knowledge base that may consist of basic skills, content knowledge, and general pedagogical skills, teaching could be trivialized and its complexities might be ignored. So a teacher has to "know the territory" of teaching (p. 9).

To sum up, the author now comes to believe that reflection, reflective thinking or reflectivity which results from the individual or collaborative efforts to think reflectively represents nothing other than an aesthetic sense for style as expressed in the following passage from Alfred N. Whitehead's *The Aims of Education*:

> Finally, there should grow the most austere of all mental qualities; I mean the sense for style. It is an aesthetic sense, based on admiration for the direct attainment of a foreseen end, simply and without waste. Style in art, style in literature, style in science, style in logic, style in practical execution have fundamentally the same aesthetic qualities, namely, attainment and restraint. The love of a subject in itself and for itself, where it is not the sleepy pleasure of pacing a mental quarter-deck, is the love of style as manifested in that study. Here we are brought back to the position from which we started, the utility of education. Style, in its finest sense, is the last acquirement of the educated mind; it is also the most useful. It pervades the whole being. The administrator with a sense for style hates waste; the engineer with a sense for style economizes his material; the artisan with a sense for style prefers good work. Style is the ultimate morality of mind (Cahn, 1970, pp. 272-273).

A similar voice is resounding in the Confucian literature called *Da Xue* [The Great Learning]. It asserts that the great learner is one who rests in "the highest excellence" and who with careful deliberation comes to "know what is first and what is last":

> WHAT THE GREAT LEARNING teaches, is to illustrate illustrious virtue; to renovate the people; and to rest in the highest excellence. The point where to rest being known, the object of pursuit is then determined; and, that being determined, a calm unperturbedness may be attained to. To that calmness there will succeed a tranquil repose. In that repose there may be careful deliberation, and that deliberation will be followed by the attainment of the desired end. Things have their root and their branches. Affairs have their end and their beginning. To know what is first and what is last will lead near to what is taught in the Great Learning (p. 1).

2.2 The Knowledge Base and the Dispositions

Reflective teaching is based on a discourse called reflection. As it has already been discussed, reflection is a word with rich historicity. It is rooted in the teaching of Socrates, especially his questioning method. The so-called "Socratic questioning" is a method that perceives things outside the self with reflection (O'Donoghue & Brooker, 1996). A variety of contemporary educational theorists including Dewey reflect this position in their work. Then, what exactly is reflection in modern thinkers? Dewey's (1933) definition of reflection was "an active, persistent, and careful consideration of any belief or supposed form of knowledge in light of the grounds supporting it and future conclusions to which it tends" (p. 6). At a general level, however, reflection or reflectivity could be summarized as follows:

(1) The spirit of inquiry or experimental spirit that leads to problem-setting and problem solving;
(2) The critical mind to guard against degenerating into "a cog in the machine" or the spirit of being an active agent as opposed to being a passive contemplator;
(3) A practical, bottom-up way of craft and/or knowledge acquisition;
(4) An elaboration of the practitioner's appreciation system along with the expansion of knowledge base;
(5) An aesthetic sense for "style" as expressed in Whitehead's "The Aims of Education" (Cahn, 1970, pp. 272-273).

Due to its historicity, the meaning of reflection can be vague but it could be epitomized in terms of two opposing yet complementary concepts: the knowledge base and the dispositions. Since the 1990s in Korea and since the 1970s in America one of the recurring themes of educational reform has been the professionalization of teaching (Huh, 1994; Jeong, 1999; Kim, Y. J., 1999; Lee, Y. S., 1999; Shulman, 1987; Van Manen, 1977). The claim has been that teaching deserves professional status. This position is assuredly linked to a premise that it should have an apparent knowledge base (Shulman, Ibid., p. 4). In the meantime, a group of educators also believe that, when it comes to reflective teaching, what matters is not the knowledge base but the dispositions of a teacher since the teacher is to develop expertise through experience and self-discipline.

In relation to this matter, there seem to exist two streams of thought in the research literature: one is that, in order to teach reflectively, there must be a body of knowledge and skill to draw on; the other is that, to be a better reflector or to be a better teacher, the dispositions of a teacher such as enthusiasm and commitment must be accounted for. These two significantly different positions on the basis of reflection and on the nature of teaching could be referred to as "Deweyan" and "Schönian." For, the perspectives of Dewey and Schön are thought to be significantly different in this matter even though they share a major portion of the definition regarding the nature of reflective teaching.

To Dewey, reflection is grounded on a universal human capacity: rational deliberative thinking. By means of which we can conceptualize alternative views on a problem and by which we are enabled to frame and reframe the problem in a variety of ways that may lead to a wider range of possible solutions and contribute to change in our personal and/or professional perspectives. Therefore, in professional training, routinization is a crucial means by which teachers become skilled enough to focus away from self and on learners. Much of our practice will be led by our established frames and routines unless and until there is good reason to reconsider them. And that is the very time that the rational deliberative thinking is required.

This view of reflection commands a host of followers: Buckley (2000); Hamilton & Pinnegar (2000); Kahne (2000); Kolb (1984); Labaree (1992 & 2000); Mahlios & Maxon (1995); Pratte & Rury (1991); Smyth (1989 & 1992); and Yost et al. (2000). Among the most prominent is Pratte & Rury (1991). Understandably, they declare that teachers belong to a group of "craft professions" different from "expert professions" (p. 125). They go on to argue that it is necessary for teachers to develop a clear consciousness of craft, namely, a faithful disposition of an artist to guide their work, and that the search for more conventional definitions of professional status are unlikely to help them.

According to their definition, a craft denotes an art or skill in a field or calling, and the craft people acquire and develop a sense of craft or a conscience of craft. In developing the conscience of craft, the concept of community is important and the mastery of technique in communal contexts promotes self-esteem. One may take the woodworking skill of a carpenter for an example. As the excellence in woodworking makes a carpenter a good craftsperson, so a teacher is best evaluated in the action of teaching. For this reason, as they contend, it is problematic for external authorities to impose meaningful standards of performance on teaching. They assert that teachers are best judged by other teachers. Kazumasa Arita (1989), among many teachers, would be the first to agree on this view, for he says that he has worked hard to be a *meijin* [master craftsman] of teaching all his working life.

In the meantime, Schönian thinkers such as Ben-Peretz (2001); Ethell & McMeniman (2000); Gorrell & Capran (1989); Lieberman (2000); Ross (1989); Shulman (1987); Tom (1997); and Wallace (1991) would believe that the reflection should be grounded on the expert practitioner's knowledge base even if the epistemological system for that knowledge base is quite elusive in nature. Especially what Schön called reflection-in-action, that is, a spontaneous reflection in the midst of action, is valued most here because it engages the practitioner in reflection to guide the real-time reframing and on-the-spot experiment. So, for fostering the development of reflection Ross (1989) suggests strategies including 1) communicating that knowledge is socially constructed; 2) modeling reflection; and 3) providing guided practice in reflective thinking and teaching (p. 23).

Interestingly, Shulman (1987) identifies the knowledge base with the following category headings:

Chart 1 Categories of Teacher's Knowledge Base

- content knowledge
- general pedagogical knowledge, with special reference to those broad principles and strategies of classroom management and organization that appear to transcend subject matter
- curriculum knowledge, with particular grasp of the materials and programs that serve as "tools of the trade" for teachers
- pedagogical content knowledge, that special amalgam of content and pedagogy that is uniquely the province of teachers, their own special form of professional understanding
- knowledge of learners and their characteristics
- knowledge of educational contexts, ranging from the workings of the group or classroom, the governance and financing of school districts, to the character of communities and cultures
- knowledge of educational ends, purposes, and values, and their philosophical and historic grounds

The first five categories relate to a teacher's personal development while the last two categories address the need for his or her social development. It is also noteworthy that the 'pedagogical content knowledge' is referred to as "uniquely the province of teachers."

Teaching, English language teaching included, is both an activity which requires a personal commitment and a profession which requires a sturdy knowledge base. It draws on human integrity interacting with experience. Straightforwardness and honesty to self are prerequisites. For, these qualities will lead the language teachers to accurately frame their current situations without the addition or the subtraction, identify the problem areas, and effectively reframe them to find some solutions. The reflective process, however, could hardly be possible in a vacuum; without the conscience of craft, without the proper appreciation system, without the knowledge base, a reflective problem-posing or a reasonable problem-solving would not take place. Therefore, it follows that both Deweyan and Schönian view of reflection are crucial to understanding the nature of reflective teaching and/or thinking.

2.3 Models of Enhancing Reflectivity in Teaching

During the past thirty years or so, reflective practice and the value of reflectivity have been common research themes in the field of teaching in the western world (Gabel, 2001; Roth, 1989; Schön, 1987; Smyth, 1989; Zeichner & Liston, 1987). Needless to say, this current revival owes much to Dewey's insight and his idea of liberal progressive education. In this section the researcher will examine recent developments of the reflective thinking focusing on their models of promoting reflectivity among teachers and teacher educators. As will be seen shortly, the models proposed and discussed by theorists and researchers are diversified and the ways and extent of implementation are dynamic and far-reaching although they fall short of theoretical scrupulosity or of the appropriateness to Korean EFL contexts.

First of all, Van Manen (1977) conceived of reflection as a progression involving three distinct stages. The first concerns the effective application of skills and technical knowledge in the classroom setting. The second stage involves reflection about the assumptions underlying a specific classroom practice as well as the consequences of that practice on student learning. At this level of reflection teachers are assessing the educational implications of their actions and beliefs. The third stage entails questioning the moral and ethical dimensions of decisions related, directly or indirectly, to the classroom situation. Here, teachers make connections between situations they encounter and the broader social, political, and economic forces that influence those events.

This three-stage model of Van Manen summarized as 1) the stage of analyzing strategies; 2) the stage of reflection on assumptions; and 3) the stage of reflection on moral and ethical variables surely is an important insight. However, it mainly consists of teaching and reflection with no proper consideration of planning. Considering that planning is a crucial component of any teaching, it should not be taken for granted in modeling a reflective practice. In this respect, Richards & Lockhart's (1994) action research model seems more appropriate. Their action research project consists of five stages: 1) initial reflection; 2) planning; 3) action; 4) observation; and 5) reflection. But the relationship between initial reflection and planning is rather ambiguous and observation will likely cause practical difficulties since the teacher has to observe his own classroom while teaching.

On the other hand, Wallace (1991) integrates two sources of knowledge, received knowledge and experiential knowledge, with practice. His reflective practice model of professional development is highly recommended by Nunan (2001, pp. 197-207). In developing his own model, Wallace begins by examining some current models of teacher education: 1) the craft model; 2) the applied science model; and 3) the reflective model. And he goes on to describe the notion of teacher as "reflective practitioner." He shows how the notion of "reflective practitioner" can provide a coherent framework which links educational theory and practice. Mostly he explores ways in which a reflective approach can be applied to areas of the language teacher education program.

The Reflective Practice Model that Wallace finally came up with looks like Figure 1.

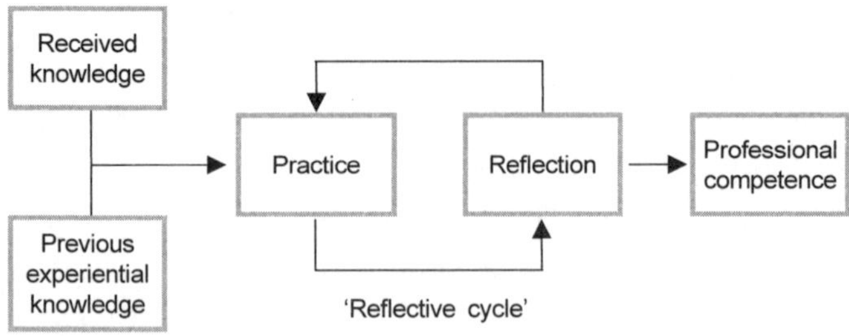

Figure 1 Reflective Practice Model Proposed by Wallace*
*Adapted from Wallace (1991), p. 15.

This model has an apparent strength in that it gives due recognition to the elements of received knowledge and experiential knowledge which may cover the craft and the knowledge of applied science. However, the drawback is its lack of consideration of the reflective practitioner's dispositions. By and large, it is a Schönian model so that it fails to incorporate the Deweyan conception of reflective teaching, that is, the positive influence of the beliefs and attitudes of a reflective practitioner.

Ross (1989), on the other hand, shows her concern with the developmental stages of reflective practice of preservice teachers. She describes and evaluates the efforts of a teacher educator to introduce teacher effectiveness research to preservice teachers in ways that support the development of critical reflection. She thus introduces a seven-stage development model for student teachers' reflective judgment. Chart 2 will show how the student teachers' reflective judgement can be developed step by step, evolving from a single, fixed perspective toward rich, balanced perspectives:

As the stages move up to the higher ones, development of reflective thinking among the teachers entails development of their attitudes and abilities and that the most important requirement of mature reflectivity is the ability to view situations

Chart 2 Stages in the Development of Reflective Judgment[1]

The Individual:

Stages 1 and 2
- Views world as simple
- Believes knowledge to be absolute
- Views authorities as the source of all knowledge

Stage 3
- Acknowledges existence of differences of viewpoints
- Believes knowledge to be relative
- Sees varying positions about issues as equally right or equally wrong
- Uses unsupported personal belief as frequently as "hard" evidence in making decisions
- Views truths as "knowable" but not yet known

Stage 4
- Perceives legitimate differences of viewpoint
- Develops a beginning ability to interpret evidence
- Uses unsupported personal belief and evidence in making decisions but its beginning to be able to differentiate between them
- Believe that knowledge is uncertain in some areas

Stages 5 and 6
- Views knowledge as contextually based
- Develops views that an integrated perspective can be evaluated as more or less likely to be true
- Develops initial ability to integrate evidence into a coherent point of view

Stage 7
- Exhibits all characteristics listed in stages 5 and 6
- Possesses ability to make objective judgments based on reasoning and evidence
- Is able to modify judgments based on new evidence if necessary

from multiple perspectives. It is easy to see her making efforts to incorporate the dispositions of the preservice teachers in designing the reflective practice model. However, the main drawback is that the supposed operation of the reflective stages is rather linear with no consideration of their possible cyclical nature.

Roth (1989) considers the cyclical nature of reflective teaching. He introduces and reviews the four models of re-

[1] Ross, 1989, p. 25.

flective practice to find an operational definition of the term "reflective practitioner." According to him, the processes in which the reflective practitioner engages are: 1) the process of inquiry; 2) the behavioristic model; 3) the personalistic model; and 4) the traditional-craft model. This emphasizes the accumulation of the wisdom of experienced practitioners. He describes the first model as essential to the reflective practitioner, but his ultimate preference is the fifth alternative, namely, the dialectic model in the process of which teachers reflect, make decisions, test and revise with ever more deepening understanding of his instructional practice. The dialectic model indeed has cyclicity in its conceptual operation, but his final remark is that this is not so much a cyclical process as it is a spiral, with one set of experiences and decisions building on the previous ones.

By and large, Roth's model is not a static one. It is a dynamic process which is "always becoming." Compared to the models of Van Manen (1977), Ross (1989), and Wallace (1991), it seems that Roth's due focus on cyclicity is a significant development in defining the characteristics of a proper reflection process. His model, however, lacks originality—it is adapted from the works of earlier researchers Kitchener (1977) and King (1977)—and specificity. As a result, the teachers who want to be reflective practitioners cannot get the full implication of cyclicity when they try implementing his model in their teaching.

Henderson's (1989) postmodern approach named "positioned reflective practice (PRP)" is also insubstantial and vague. His interpretive analysis of the relationship between language and meaning leads to an understanding that our discourse has a formative, constitutive effect on reality and that whatever we perceive takes place through the act of language. But with this philosophical understanding alone, we cannot get the actual job done either at school or in the classroom.

With an acerbic attitude toward the background of the emergence of reflectivity as a conceptual thrust, Smyth (1989) discusses the impediments to empowerment that teachers and teacher educators confront. He argues that if teachers are going to uncover the forces that inhibit and constrain them, they need to engage in four forms of action with respect to teaching. These "forms" are characterized by four sequential stages and are linked to a series of questions: 1) describing (What do I do?); 2) informing (What does this mean?); 3) confronting (How did I come to be like this?); and 4) reconstructing (How might I do things differently?).

Smyth (1992) addresses the problem of educational politics by arranging his position in four ways. First, the rhetoric of going back to practitioner forms of knowledge may not entirely altruistic as it displays significant moves to bolster centralized bureaucracy. Second, the contradiction is only explainable when we look at wider structural adjustments—such as "free marketeering"—currently occurring in Western capitalist systems (p. 269). Third, reflective practices may entrap them within the "New Right ideology" of radical interventionism. Finally, teacher educators should engage teachers in "untangling the complex web of ideologies that surround them in their teaching" for a better social, cultural, political reflective approach (p. 295).

His bitterly critical view of the political background of the booming concern in reflective practice is of much value to anyone who deals with the nature of reflective teaching. However, it must not be overlooked that there is an inherent healing effect in reflectivity. Even if the general call to reflective practice might have come from the "New Right ideology," there seems to be no other way of breaking this link at the moment except that teachers make the most of their reflective potentials to fight back the conspiracy.

Most researchers discussed so far have dealt with the problem of increasing reflectivity in the general educational setting. It is hardly a surprise considering that the idea of reflective teaching originally came from the discourse on general education and moved later on to teacher education. In this context, Roberts (1997) seems to have made a significant contribution to applying the general conception of reflective teaching to the field of language teaching. He starts by examining the foundations of language teacher education and then gives advice on initial teacher education and on inservice education and training for the teachers and providers in charge. His strengths lie in the application of the main theories of human learning to the education of language teachers. Drawing on a social constructivist perspective, Roberts suggests a framework for planning preservice and inservice programs, and illustrates it with case studies from a range of language teacher training situations around the world.

To sum up, the western literature relating to the models of reflection and reflectivity seems to have retained a persistent theme: the need for intervention in the reflective processes that foster the development of novice or expert teachers' knowledge-in-action. It appears essential that teachers be involved in some form of reflective inquiry to develop an understanding of what takes place in their classroom where the job of teaching is actually being done. The ways of implementing this are largely dependent on Schönian or Deweyan thought. However, the proposed reflective practices differ from researcher to researcher, from case to case. Some engage themselves in developing a proper model for reflective teaching; others concern themselves with specific ways of implementing the already defined reflective practice using such tools as portfolios and educational networks.

The problem is that, in view of the purpose of this study, there is no appropriate model to be adapted to Korean English education. Some models are too local or specific to be of any help while others are too general or vague to be successfully implemented in Korean language teaching environment. Another problem is that, while there seems to have been a plethora of research on reflective teaching for the past thirty years in the United States and other English-spoken countries, there have been virtually no researches found in Korea that deal with the practicality of implementing reflective language teaching in any serious manner. In fact there are only a handful of papers that seem to have discussed the subject concerned either principally or peripherally. Regrettably, though, most of them have failed to attack the main body.

Joe & Matheson (1996) is the first paper that has taken up the theme of reflective language teaching as its main concern. The two English teachers describe an experience in a teacher development (TD) group that makes use of the concept of reflective teaching. They wrote teacher journals and participated in a continuing dialogue about their experiences in their own or others' classes so that they would come to a clearer understanding of what it is to be a teacher of EFL and of how they can become better at what they do. They did a lot of collective thinking and finally recommended that all teachers form development groups.

Though it falls short of "a hard science," this research should be regarded as valuable in that they showed a possible way of implementing reflective practice in a Korean educational setting. The significant weakness of this research is that it mainly takes a form of reporting back what has happened in the TD group, thus lacking any cogent theoretical basis which may add to the credibility of the research.

Another research done in relation to reflective practice is the one which deals with self-observation technique for preservice secondary teachers. Jeon & Kim (2001) explore strengths and weaknesses in the teaching of student teachers through self-observation, providing suggestions for preparation of preservice teachers for effective classroom interactions. But their study fails to deal with what the student teachers actually do before and after teaching as fledgling reflective practitioners. Self-observation alone cannot constitute a major tool for reflective teaching. In order to fully explain the phenomenon and look into the depth of reflective practice, any good study on reflective teaching must use a more principal approach to coding the complex teaching practices of the preservice or inservice teachers.

One more study related to reflective practice in a Korean EFL setting is the one conducted by Kim B.-S. (2001). She uses her reflective diary and the elementary school children's diary about learning as well as videotaped recordings of her English classes to define the effect of teacher belief system on English instruction. Maintaining that teacher beliefs should not be disregarded as it has a very strong influence on instruction, she calls for a need to do more research on the impact of children's belief on English instruction as well as on the identification of the belief system that experienced teachers have. For, she believes that especially the latter will help to determine which belief system is desirable for an English teacher. The study, however, shows little effort to establish the reflectivity in teacher beliefs and to answer how it has an impact on classroom teaching.

Conclusively, it appears that what the three of Korean

researchers have done only amounts to a peripheral touch in applying the conception of reflectivity while the Western literature mainly deals with the problems of a theoretical model development or of a particular case to the extent that they are rather general or too situation-specific to be directly introduced to our educational setting. With this crucial research gap in mind, the researcher will develop in the chapter following the next a more feasible Reflective Language Teaching (RLT) model focusing on the cyclical operation of the three modules: planning, teaching, and reflection.

2.4 Methodological Eclecticism

A full-scale RLT seeks for a teaching solution using multiple perspectives. It starts with recognizing a teaching dilemma. It responds to the dilemma, and then frames and reframes the dilemma, experimenting with it (Ross, 1989). In so doing the language teacher examines the intended and unintended consequence of an implemented solution. Dewey (1916) called this process "inquiry," "looking into things," or "investigating" (p. 114). This line of thought is a clue for the significance of a bottom-up approach in RLT. And its implication for on-the-spot language teachers is nothing less than methodological eclecticism (Clemente, 2001; Hamberger and Moore, 1997; Richards and Lockhart, 1994; Roberts, 1998; Wallace, 1991).

In English language teaching, there is no one best method or approach. And this is probably why Celce-Murcia points out that "language teaching is a field where fads and heroes have come and gone in a manner fairly consistent with the kinds of changes that occur in youth culture" (1991, p. 3). There is no panacea for problems of language teaching. In a "forked road" situation, language teachers need only to rely on their own judgment to come up with the most appropriate solution to the perceived problem. Therefore, teaching English must use eclecticism so that the solutions might be sought continuously to come up with the best approaches or methods available.

As already mentioned, the Communicative Approach is a robust teaching methodology based on a theory of language as communication. Hymes (1972) reference to "communicative competence," Firth's interactional view of language and Halliday's functional account of language use as well as Widdowson's (1978) view of the relationship between linguistic systems and their communicative values in text and discourse all contributed to this powerful methodology. A more recent method in line with this approach is the Natural Method proposed by Krashen and Terrell (1983). They contend that their attempt is to present a new approach based on a new theory of language in order to replace the Audiolingual approaches.

The two theoreticians claim that their methodology has been adequately field-tested, but there are no evidences that it was tested in Asian countries including Korea, Japan or China. Considering that it is generally more difficult for Asians to learn English than for Europeans, their claim must be used with caution. Another defect is that their theory is based on too lofty goals for us Korean learners to attain. Designing a common language course, they divide the goals according to basic personal communication skills and academic learning skills (Ibid., p. 66). Surprisingly, the "basic" oral personal communication skills include "listening to radio, television, movies, music." And the "basic" written personal communication skills include "reading advertisements" and "pleasure reading." To say the least, these are the goals for the most advanced learners of English in Korea.

Immaculate as they seem in their own theoretical construction, the varied techniques, methods and approaches have both merits and limitations, both strengths and weaknesses. And this is probably why a good selection of new post-CLT approaches to language learning are already being suggested in the ELT methodology field. Among them are Task-based Learning (TBL), and Text-based Teaching (TBT). TBL is a method proposed by the Indian scholar N. S. Prabhu in 1979. This method is built around a syllabus which contains no linguistic specifications but a series of tasks in the form of problem-solving activities. And TBT, also known as genre-based, is based on a model of text-based learning that grew out of a model of language, that is, Systemic-Functional Grammar. It is an approach where language occurs as whole texts which are embedded in the social contexts in which they are used (Paul Knight, 2001. In Candlin & Mercer (Eds.), p. 162).

These are relatively new methods. So the reflective teachers ought to know that as they are new the flaws and weaknesses have not yet been fully exposed. There are, however, older methods that have apparently gone through the test of time and that it seems easier for Korean English language teachers to adopt. Among others most prominent are Grammar-Translation Method, Audio-Lingual Method, Suggestopedia, Silent Way and Total Physical Response. Let's briefly examine the strengths and weaknesses of these methodologies of language teaching.

The Grammar-Translation Method was devised and developed for the nineteenth-century grammar school. It began in Germany, in Prussian *Gymnasien* (Howatt, 1984, p. 131). The method was so ordinary. Each lesson had one or two new grammar rules, a short vocabulary list, and some practice examples to translate. Boring, maybe, but hardly the horror story was it. The main drawback is that there is little use of the target language with the focus on grammatical parsing. And it usually required early reading of difficult literary texts. The result is usually an inability on the part of the student to use the language for oral communication. But there are also strengths: it is not expensive and the teacher does not have to be able to speak the target language to explain the complex rules or vocabularies.

Another "traditional" methodology is the Audio-Lingual Method. Despite differences, this method shares one thing with Grammar-Translation Method (Nunan, 1999, p. 77). Both separate the teaching of grammatical form from communicative meaning. Words are usually learned as individual items in lists without being contextualized. Audiolingualists believe that language learning is a process of habit formation. There are also some advantages in this manner of teaching. The two staple techniques of ALM, mimicry and memorization, are easy to implement in EFL contexts where the students scarcely have opportunities to experience "authentic" communication. And it is easily implemented in a large-sized classroom if only the audiolingual gear is to be provided properly.

Suggestopedia, Silent Way, and Total Physical Response (TPR) are the approaches that appeared as a reaction to the behaviorist features of the audiolingual approach. They share much in common in that they draw on affective and cognitive aspects of language learning. Caleb Gattengno's Silent Way focuses on learning. Production is elicited at first with the aid of "scatter charts" and Cuisenaire Rods. The learning process utilizes discovery learning where students resort to their inner resources and "inner criteria" (Celce-Murcia, 1991, p. 31). The cardinal principle is that the teacher should subordinate teaching to learning. This method is peculiarly learner-centered. And this constitutes its advantages and disadvantages in that certain types of teacher-centered instruction such as expository teaching are sometimes better used in foreign language teaching (Eggen and Kauchak, 2001, pp. 517-519).

Total Physical Response, on the other hand, is a comprehension-based approach (Celce-Murcia, 1991, p. 25). It postulates that during the preproduction period children apparently learn to understand a great deal long before they try to say much. The door of understanding is first opened as children respond meaningfully to directives. The context-clear situations invite an action response rather than a verbal response. This method of language teaching is grounded on the observation that children's early social interaction is indeed through a physical response to invitations for movement. One of the most significant merit could be that it activates the right hemisphere of the brain in language learning. However, a major criticism is that it fails to lead students to perform "survival" functions, such as exchanging greetings, asking directions, and ordering a meal (Ibid., p. 27).

Both Silent Way and TPR are especially good for teaching elementary-level students, which might mean that they are not appropriate to teaching higher-level students. But there are also cases where they are creatively adapted to intermediate learners. For instance, Rassius has made a great success in teaching French to American undergraduates by combining TPR with acting (Oller, 1993, pp. 40-49).

Suggestopedia created by Georgi Lozanov in the late 1960s is enjoying a recent revival thanks to the development of neuropsychology. Concentrating on learner receptivity, Suggestopedia uses music and complex means of relaxation to mediate states of mind in which a very large volume of material can be absorbed with ease. This "new" method was initially received with much scepticism. Now, however, various neuro-psychological discoveries support the theory and practice of Suggestopedia. For one thing, the method agrees with the knowledge that the two brain hemispheres react differently to particular stimuli, that neo-cortex functioning is inhibited by alarm and survival activity from the lower areas of the brain and that long-term memory relies heavily on circuits housed largely in the "limbic" or emotional area (Tomlinson, 1998, pp. 311-313).

Despite the revival, Suggestopedia is still regarded as a fringe method. So are the cases of Silent Way and TPR. The mainstream methods swinging their arms in Asian countries are GTM, ALM and CLT (Choi, 2000; Gorsuch, 2000; Li, 1998; Namoto et al., 2000; Shin, 2001; Wang, 1999; Wu, 2001). It should be noted, however, that the first two mainstream methodologies, namely, GTM and ALM are being shunned as "outdated" methods. Among the educators, there seems to lie a mentality that the newer the method the better it is. Whatever method the teachers use, however, the most important thing is that it should be used creatively and appropriately.

To teach creatively, the teachers should know of their students, of their subject, and of the nature of teaching. To teach appropriately, the teachers should first locate the problem areas and then frame and reframe the problems in critical reflection to find out the best solution possible. This leads nowhere but to the tenet of eclectic RLT.

III. SURVEY ON TEACHERS' BELIEFS AND ATTITUDES

3.1 Purport of the Survey Research

The society and the policy makers think that teachers are the ones who are primarily responsible for schooling although the students' right to learn precedes that of teaching in legal terms (Cf. Korea General Association of Teacher Organizations, 1998, p. 3). To them, the problem of English education is the problem of English teacher. It seems quite a natural postulation in that the efforts of the teachers on hour-to-hour basis accumulate daily and finally amount to a colossal form of national education. Their hard work and pains, however, have been rarely appreciated by the students, by parents, by administrators, or even by themselves. To help them develop insight into a battery of techniques which can be used to rethink their practice, any designer of a teacher-helping model has to find out about how to tap on these elusive aspects of teacher development.

Therefore, a study of developing a teacher-helping model should involve teacher beliefs. Otherwise, the resulting model or suggestions to teaching reflectively could be another failing case of a top-down approach to teacher development as in the United States, Caribbean or Japanese cases (Green, 2000; Jennings, 2001; Labaree, 1992; Namoto et al., 2000; Tom, 1997). The main purpose of the survey is thus to find out what exactly the teachers think of themselves, of their job, and of their wants and needs; what attitudes they have toward schools and administrative systems; finally, what beliefs or inclinations they have toward the idea of implementing reflective teaching.

3.2 Method

3.2.1 Participants

The participants in this survey involved 50 preservice and 38 inservice teachers. The demographic characteristics of the participants are as follows:

As shown in Table 1, the demographic composition of the participants was attempted to be as diverse as possible and the sampling was done as randomly as possible. Agewise there are ample variations while genderwise females outnumber males

Table 1 Demographic Features of Participants

Service	School	Number of Persons	Gender	Age
Preservice	undergraduate	35	F: 32, M: 3	19~27
	graduate	15	F: 11, M: 4	25~43
Inservice	highschool	20	F: 5, M: 15	24~57
	middle school	14	F: 12, M: 15	34~55
	elementary school	4	F: 4	24~39
Total		88	F: 64, M: 24	19~57

nearly by the ratio of 2.7: 1. These two variables, age and gender, will not be of much interest in the following analysis. The preservice-inservice variable, instead, will be considered as a main population parameter. For some realistic reasons, however, the demography of the preservice teachers were limited to the students at a local university in Seoul and inservice teachers from other provinces than Seoul, Keonggi, Chungnam, and Jeonbuk were not included.

3.2.2 Instrumentation

All the subjects were given a survey questionnaire developed by the researcher based on a review of the literature on general pedagogy, TESL methodology, and reflective teaching as well as on the researcher's teaching experience. Data was collected either by personal contact or by e-mail and the data collection was done between November, 2001 and January, 2002.

The instrument consisted of 48 questions under four main categories as presented in Table 2. Individual items of each category are provided in the Appendix I, translated from Korean into English.

Table 2 Contents of the Questionnaire

Main Categories	Items	Type of Response
I. View of teaching	1. It's a canonical profession 2. One of the most popular jobs 3. I'm respected by students 4. I'm what I wanted to be 5. Teacher has no autonomy 6. There's developmental stage	5-point Likert-type scale

	7. The greatest impediment 8. How advanced am I? 9. Requirement for expert 10. Reason to be a teacher	multiple-choice response
II. Educational philosophy & view of ideal teacher	1. We need traditional trinity 2. Teacher is a partner 3. Behavior by design 4. Teacher is a mere helper 5. I have humanistic concerns 6. Teacher as cultural mediator 7. The ideal of hongik-ingan 8. Teacher role to be changed 9. Ideal-reality gap 10. Should include social issues	5-point Likert-type scale
	11. The most important quality 12. Ideal teacher for Korean ELT	multiple-choice response
III. Classroom behavior	1. I give students much autonomy 2. I value individual difference 3. I receive a lot of feedback 4. I've used TPR 5. I've used games 6. I've used the Internet 7. I've used computer courseware 8. Automatic habit is important 9. It's necessary to use discipline 10. I have various strategies	5-point Likert-type scale
	11. Urgent need for better teacher 12. Least proficient skill 13. Type of teacher that I am	multiple-choice response
IV. Reflective self-development	1. Do you reflect on your teaching? 2. Experience in reflective journal 3. Experience in teacher stories 4. I visit web sites quite often 5. Talking with others about ELT 6. Critical reflection will be helpful 7. I understand student culture 8. Teachers develop collaboratively 9. Enthusiasm for workshops 10. School culture influences TD	5-point Likert-type scale
	11. Urgent need to improve ITE 12. Present method for reflection 13. Desirable method for reflection	multiple-choice response

3.2.3 Analysis

For data analysis of the present study, descriptive and inferential statistics were used, with calculations performed via the SPSS 7.0 Version for Windows. Descriptive statistics included frequencies, minimum/maximum statistics, central tendency (mean) and variability (standard deviation and skewness) to organize, summarize and analyze the data from the respondents.

Inferential statistics were used to determine the behavior and the relationship of the random variables of the sample population. One-Way ANOVA was done to compare the variance of the quantitative dependent variables such as Likert-type questionnaire items and a single factor (independent) variable like preservice/inservice division. These analyses of variance were used to test the null hypothesis that the means of both groups are equal. The probability levels that resulted from this analysis of variance were the same with the results of the two-samples t-tests. Therefore, t-tests were excluded altogether in any analysis of the data.

Correlation among the statistics of some questionnaire items was calculated but there was hardly any statistical significance found, so its statistics were not analyzed. Chi-squared distribution was also investigated in the crosstabulation to examine respondent variables and content variables, but its statistics were not specified except for the special case. Against the results of the questionnaire items, the descriptive statistics were given for each respondent variable and then, to determine whether there is any significant difference between the preservice and inservice sample population, the One-Way ANOVA test was administered. According to the results of this inferential statistics, the crosstabulation for each of the questionnaire item that turned out to have a significant difference was pursued before the results were analyzed and discussed. In the interpretation of the results, the level of statistical significance is p=.05.

3.3 Results and Discussion

Before summarizing and analyzing the statistical results, the author will first examine the responses to the questionnaire items in clusters and categories one by one.

3.3.1 View of Teaching

Under the first category, there are 6 Likert-type items which asked: 1) "Is the job of a teacher among such major professions as that of a doctor, a lawyer, or an architect?" 2) "Is the job of teaching one of the most popular jobs nowadays?" 3) "Are you respected by your students?" 4) "Are you the teacher that you have wanted to be?" 5) "Do you think teachers have no autonomy at all?" and 6) "Is there a developmental stage for a teacher?"

As shown in Table 3, the participants responded positively to all of the items except for the first item.

Among the positive responses, however, the response to the fifth item should be considered as another negative response in that the content of the item statement is negatively presented, namely: "Teachers have no autonomy at all; every decision is made by outside conditions and social policies."

The response to item number 1 is negative with the mean score

Table 3 Descriptive Statistics for Items I. 1-6

	Minimum	Maximum	Mean	Std.	Skewness
	Statistic	Statistic	Statistic	Statistic	Statistic
1. Major profession	1	5	2.32	1.13	.661
2. Most popular job	1	5	3.32	1.01	.001
3. Teacher respected	1	5	3.58	.77	.115
4. Teacher that I wanted to be	2	5	3.93	.84	-.462
5. Teacher has no autonomy	1	5	3.07	1.08	.309
6. Development stage	1	5	3.45	1.04	-.632

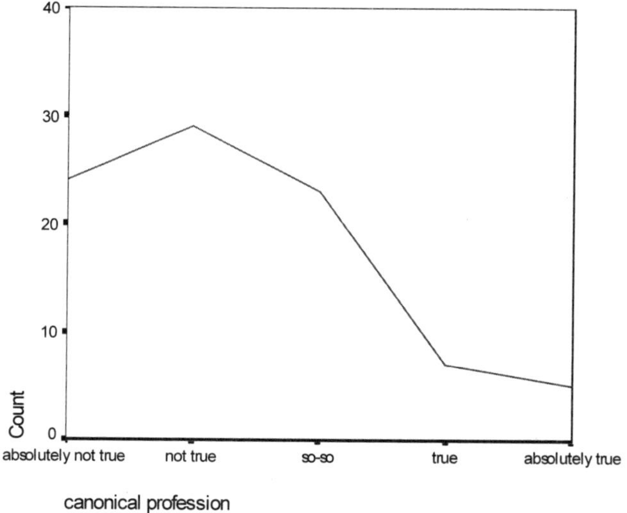

Figure 2 Skewness of Item I. 1

2.32, and the statistic shows a strongly positively skewed distribution[1] as shown in Figure 2; on the contrary, the response

[1] Skewness is a measure of the asymmetry of a distribution. The normal distribution is symmetric, and has a skewness value of zero. A distribution with a significant positive skewness has a long right tail. A distribution with a significant negative skewness has a long left tail. If the statistic is positively skewed, it implies that there are more negative answers than positive whereas if the statistic is negatively skewed, it means that there are more positive answers to the given question.

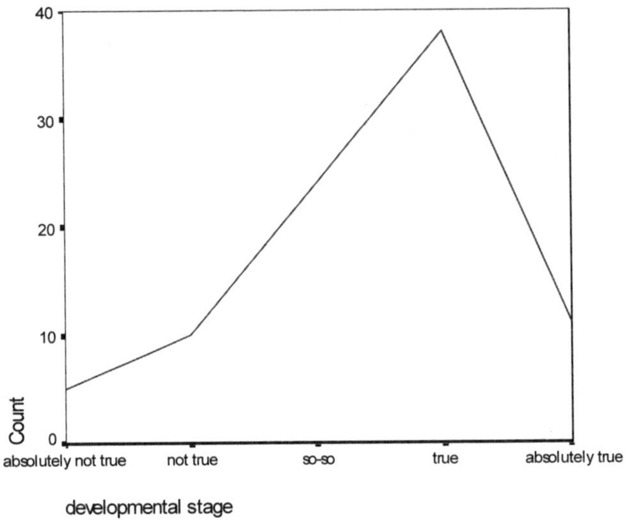

Figure 3 Skewness of Item I. 6

to item number 6 is positive with the mean score 3.45, and the statistic shows a rather negatively skewed distribution as shown in Figure 3.

In order to determine whether there is any significant difference in responding the above questionnaire items between preservice and inservice sample population, the One-Way ANOVA test was administered and the obtained F scores and probability levels are as follows:

All the mean differences between preservice and inservice teachers are the results of random chance except for the second and the third item. The mean differences between preservice and inservice teachers in these items are statistically significant. Let's see the Crosstabulation[2] in Table 5 and 6.

---

[2] Crosstabulation is a table displaying the number of cases falling into each combination of the categories of two or more categorical variables. The

Table 4 One-Way ANOVA for Items I. 1-6

Items	Variable Type	df	Mean quare	F	Sig.
1. Major profession	between groups	1	3.828	3.069	.083
2. Most popular job	between groups	1	10.548	11.549	.001**
3. Teacher respected	between groups	1	2.981	5.290	.024*
4. Teacher that I wanted to be	between groups	1	1.902	2.741	.101
5. No autonomy	between groups	1	2.542	2.208	.141
6. Developmental stage	between groups	1	.075	.69	.794

Table 5 Crosstabulation of Item I. 2

count

		2. most popular job					Total
		absolutely not true	not true	so-so	true	absolutely true	
service	preservice		6	17	17	10	50
	inservice	2	11	15	8	2	38
Total		2	17	32	25	12	88

Table 6 Crosstabulation of Item I. 3

count

		3. teacher respected					Total
		absolutely not true	not true	so-so	true	absolutely true	
service	preservice			22	19	9	50
	inservice	1	1	21	13	2	38
Total		1	1	43	32	11	88

To go further, as shown in Table 7, to the questionnaire item 7 asking what would be the greatest impediment in the

---

counts of cases are often supplemented or replaced by percentages of various kinds. The skewness, frequencies, and percentages of the rest of the items in the first category, all of which are multiple choices, are shown in Table 6.

professional development of a teacher, the second choice "stress from identity crisis" received the most tallies. This could be interpreted as an expression of dissatisfaction with the present school situation and teaching environment. In his article, "A Study on the Reality and the Ideal of Schooling," Chung (1998) points out that Korean schools are suffering from the three inveterate ills: 1) education focused on entrance examination; 2) loss in sense of community; and 3) selfish competition. This sort of dark side of our school culture may have impact on the perception of the teachers when they think about their profession. And this is probably why the respondents marked on the fifth choice, "bad educational conditions" the second most to the question "What is the greatest impediment?"

As for the skewness, the statistics of the first two items are

Table 7 Descriptive Statistics for Items I. 7-10

Items	Choices	Frequency	Percent	Skewness
7. Greatest impediment	• alienation from society	2	2.3	.180
	• stress from identity crisis	32	36.4	
	• conflict with administrators	4	4.5	
	• budget deficiency	16	18.2	
	• bad educational conditions	28	31.8	
	• deficiency in consolidation	2	2.3	
	• others	4	4.5	
8. How advanced am I?	• novice	30	34.1	.666
	• average	46	52.3	
	• advanced	10	11.4	
	• superlative	2	2.3	
9. Requirement for expert	• linguistics & pedagogy	2	2.3	-.333
	• English proficiency	13	14.8	
	• motivating techniques	25	28.4	
	• love for students	17	19.4	
	• hard work for good teaching	31	35.2	
10. Reason for becoming an English teacher	• perceived social status	13	14.8	-.564
	• stable salary	9	10.2	
	• enough leisure time	20	22.7	
	• pleasurable school life	35	39.8	
	• others	11	12.5	

Table 8 Crosstabulation for Item I.

count

		8. How advanced am I?				Total
		novice	average	advanced	superlative	
service	preservice	29	17	4		50
	inservice	1	29	6	2	38
Total		30	46	10	2	88

positive with the second item more skewed than the first. This means that the answers to the questionnaire item 8 are more or less concentrated on the first two choices. The frequencies also show this tendency clearly with the values 30 and 46 for 'novice' and 'average' respectively. The skewness of the other two items shows negative value with the first item less skewed than the second. This means that the majority of the answers to the questionnaire item 10 is to be found among the last three choices. Namely, this shows that the respondents think 'enough leisure time,' 'pleasurable school life,' and 'others' to be the more probable reasons for the question why they became or will become an English teacher.

To the questionnaire item 8, majority of the respondents answered on "average." As the crosstabulation of Table 8 tells us, even a good number of the preservice teachers think of themselves as average. Only two of the inservice teachers responded that they are superlative.

On the other hand, there were 16 answers written by respondents who were not satisfied with the answer choices specified in the questionnaire. Among them one answer is related to Item 1, four answers are related to Item 7, and eleven answers are related to Item 10 as seen below:

Chart 3 Other Answers for View of Teaching

Toward Item I. 1: "I think the present social status of English teachers is equal to that of a major profession such as doctor, lawyer and architect," an undergraduate student said: "For women it is regarded as prestigious, but for men it is a different story."

Toward Item I. 7: "What do you think is the greatest impediment in the professional development of an English teacher?" an undergraduate student answered: "each individual teacher's lack of will to develop." Another undergraduate student answered: "the trend of appearance of a growing number of students who have already had both experience in foreign culture and a good command of English." A graduate student answered: "the tendency of falling into mannerism." A middle school teacher in Seoul answered: "lack of opportunities to recharge our batteries."

Toward Item I. 10: "What is the reason you became or will become an English teacher?" an undergraduate student said: "It's been my career goal since young." Another undergraduate student said: "Because there is comparatively less gender discrimination." Another undergraduate student said: "Teaching is such a good profession that the growth of the individual students I teach could be my biggest reward." A graduate student answered: "Just because I have wanted to be." A high school teacher in Seoul said: "Well, . . ." Another high school teacher in Seoul answered: "Compatibility with other professions in society." A high school teacher in Keonggi said: "I can continue studying." Another high school teacher in Keonggi said: "In order to follow the example of my father." A high school teacher in Jeonbuk said: "Because I like English." A middle school teacher in Chungnam said: "All four choices should be my answer."

As shown in Table 7 above, teachers believe that hard work for good teaching is the most urgent need for the professional competency and that motivating techniques are the second most important skill they ought to have for their development. This response indirectly shows that, at least, they don't think teaching is an easy job to do. To the question, "Why did you become or wish to become an English teacher?" the most favorite answer was "pleasurable school life," followed by "enough leisure time" as the second most.

To sum up, teachers generally believe: 1) that their job is popular though it is hardly commensurate with the job of a doctor or a lawyer; 2) that they are respected by their students; 3) that they have become what they wanted to be; 4) that, though they have little autonomy, they somehow develop stage by stage and they have to work hard to be a good teacher; 5) that they see the identity crisis as the greatest impediment for their development; 6) that they mostly think they are average teachers; and finally, 7) that they became or will become an English teacher for pleasurable school life and enough leisure time. On a closer look, however, there are ironies found in the responses to the Category I questions: first, how is it that most of the teachers are respected by students at the same time that they confess that they are going through an identity crisis?; second, how is it that they think of hard work as the most important thing in good teaching at the same time that they confess that they went into teaching for enough leisure time and pleasurable school life? As for now, suffice it to say that the conditions where teachers are situated are complicated.

3.3.2 Educational Philosophy and View of Ideal Teacher

Under the second category, there are 10 Likert-type items which asked: 1) if the traditional idea of king-teacher-father trinity should still hold good; 2) if the relationship between a teacher and learners is essentially that of collaboration; 3) if desirable human behavior is not the product of contingency but of design; 4) if teachers are a mere assistant so that students may select the appropriate programs and be made responsible for their attainment of goals; 5) if, as a teacher, you are much concerned with self, love, being, spontaneity, creativity, game, humor, naturalness, friendliness, etc.; 6) if an English teacher is the cultural mediator who is apt to bridge the gap between traditional and western culture; 7) if an English teacher should be aware that children should grow into a *hongik-ingan* [beneficent human] who will contribute to the establishment of a democratic society; 8) if the role of an English teacher ought to be changed as the society changes; 9) if there is a big gap as yet between what you are and what you want to be as a teacher; 10) if English classrooms have to cover such controversial current issues as war, drug abuse, capital punishment, and environmental protection to increase the awareness of these matters.

As shown in Table 9, most of the participants responded positively, especially to the items 2, 4, 5, and 8.

Responses to Items 1, 6, and 7 show relatively low score of mean, which means that the respondents do not entirely agree with the statements given. The statistics of skewness are also mostly high except for the Items 6, 7 and 10. This also means that the answers to these items are scattered more or less. The most concentrated tendency of responses is shown in Item 8 where the statistic soars up to -1.360.

In order to determine whether there is any significant difference in responding the above questions between preservice

Table 9 Descriptive Statistics for Items II. 1-10

	Minimum	Maximum	Mean	Std. Deviation	Skewness
	Statistic	Statistic	Statistic	Statistic	Statistic
1. Traditional trinity	1	5	3.31	1.07	-.413
2. Collaborating partner	2	5	4.20	.73	-.883
3. Behavior by design	1	5	3.90	.88	-.714
4. Teacher as helper	2	5	4.31	.75	-.909
5. Humanistic view	1	5	4.17	.81	-.997
6. Cultural mediator	1	5	3.31	.94	-.059
7. Hongik-ingan ideology	1	5	3.43	.88	.161
8. Changing roles of a teacher	1	5	4.24	.77	-1.360
9. Teacher's perceived gap	2	5	3.80	.87	-.222
10. Covering social issues	2	5	3.72	.88	-.019

Table 10 One-Way ANOVA for Items II. 1-10

Items	Variable Type	df	Mean Square	F	Sig.
1. Traditional trinity	Between Groups	1	5.957	5.523	.021*
2. Collaborating partner	Between Groups	1	.028	.051	.821
3. Behavior by design	Between Groups	1	.700	.893	.347
4. Teacher as helper	Between Groups	1	2.054	3.785	.055
5. Humanistic view	Between Groups	1	5.084	8.513	.004**
6. Cultural mediator	Between Groups	1	4.953	5.935	.017*
7. Hongik-ingan ideology	Between Groups	1	2.669	3.535	.063
8. Changing roles of teacher	Between Groups	1	.053	.088	.768
9. Teacher's perceived gap	Between Groups	1	.002	.003	.956
10. Covering social issues	Between Groups	1	.667	.853	.358

and inservice sample population, the One-Way ANOVA test was also administered and the obtained F scores and probability levels are shown in Table 10.

All the mean differences between preservice and inservice teachers are the results of random chance except for the three items: the first, fifth and sixth. The mean differences between preservice and inservice teachers in these items have turned out statistically significant. Let's see the Crosstabulation in Table 11 to see how different their tallies are.

Much to our surprise, both groups of teachers responded positively to the first item asking if we need a traditional view of teacher with the highest scores on the "true" slot; however, the student teachers agreed less with "absolutely true." It is

Table 11 Crosstabulation of Items II. 1, 5 & 6

count

		1. Traditional trinity					Total
		absolutely not true	not true	so-so	true	absolutely true	
service	preservice	5	8	17	18	2	50
	inservice	1	4	12	13	8	38
Total		6	12	29	31	10	88

count

		5. Humanistic view					Total
		absolutely not true	not true	so-so	true	absolutely true	
service	preservice			4	23	23	50
	inservice	1	1	9	17	10	38
Total		1	1	13	40	33	88

count

		6. Cultural mediator					Total
		absolutely not true	not true	so-so	true	absolutely true	
service	preservice	2	8	27	9	4	50
	inservice		6	9	18	5	38
Total		2	14	36	27	9	88

quite evident, though surprising, that both groups of teachers support the idea of teacher as a moral paragon and as a person with the same authority as a king or a parent. As to the humanistic concerns, the preservice teachers are more eager to say yes, so much so that the F value is 8.513 with the probability level of .004. When it comes to the debatable idea of teacher as a cultural mediator, the inservice teachers are far more eager to say "yes" while their younger counterparts remain less sure, preferring to stay in limbo with the majority on the "so-so" slot.

The skewness, frequencies, and percentages of the rest of the items in the second category are shown in Table 12. To the question "What do you think is the most important quality

Table 12 Descriptive Statistics for Items II. 11-12

Items	Choices	Frequency	Percent	Skewness
11. Most important quality	• integrity as an educator	1	1.1	.725
	• erudite knowledge of English	21	23.9	
	• classroom teaching techniques	17	19.3	
	• enthusiasm and commitment	49	55.7	
	• others	0	0	
12. Ideal teacher for Korean ELT	• an austere scholar-like teacher	0	0	.204
	• a charismatic teacher armed with historical awareness	5	5.7	
	• a culture-developing teacher	54	61.4	
	• a democratic teacher	28	31.8	
	• others	1	1.1	

that an English teacher should have?" the majority of teachers responded by picking "enthusiasm for and commitment to teaching." And to the question "Which of the following is the image of an ideal teacher for the improvement of Korean ELT?" even a greater number of respondents answered "a culture-developing teacher" would do. There was little difference found between the preservice and inservice teachers in responding to these questions; they are largely of the same opinion on these matters.

To sum up, the respondents seem to be in support of a traditional view of teacher authority in that they responded positively to the suggestion that the traditional idea of king-teacher-father trinity should still hold good. Ironically, however, they also gave their support to the more modern idea of teacher as a collaborating partner and to the idea of teacher as a helper. Still more ironical is their perception that, as the society changes, the role of an English teacher ought to be changed as well. Our beliefs and attitudes toward the job of teaching seem to revolve around a vast amount of complexity. Otherwise, there will be no way of explaining this phenomenon of conflicting thoughts. One more interesting irony is found in the contradiction that those who are in support of the constructivist and humanistic ideas of teaching as shown in Items II. 2, II. 4, and II. 5 do not even slightly hesitate to support the purely behavioristic conception of learning/teaching as expressed in Item II. 3 and Item III. 8 which asked if acquiring an automatic linguistic habit through repetition drills is important in learning English. The conception of teaching and learning among these teachers and language learners is so richly eclectic and complex that any theoretician will have a hard time explaining.

The preservice teachers answered somewhat differently in responding to the first, fifth, and sixth item. They are relatively less traditional, more humanistic, and less concerned with cultural education. A probable reason for the last tendency could be that they, being the members of a new generation, feel less alienated from western culture. Both the preservice and inservice teachers looked upon the quality of enthusiasm and commitment as the most important for an excellent teacher and equated a culture-developing teacher with an ideal teacher for Korean ELT.

3.3.3 Classroom Behavior

Under the third category, there are 10 Likert-type items which asked: 1) if you give considerable opportunity to students in and outside of the classroom; 2) if you usually teach students in consideration of their individual difference; 3) if you usually get a lot of feedback from students including questions, complaints and appreciations; 4) if you have taught English using TPR(Total Physical Response); 5) if you have taught English using a game; 6) if you have taught English utilizing the Internet; 7) if you have taught English using a computer courseware; 8) if you believe that acquiring an automatic linguistic habit through repetition drills is important; 9) if teachers should intercept the delinquency of a student in order to keep the concentration intact; and 10) if you can apply whatever method it is, be it individualized teaching, small-group activity, big-group activity, or multimedia lesson.

As shown in Table 13, the participants responded positively to all of the questionnaire items, except for the fourth, sixth, and seventh item.

The relatively low mean score of item 4 is due to the fact that the lack of experience of the preservice student teachers was reflected on the calculation; however, in the case of two other items, that is, 6 and 7, the mean scores of the inservice teachers' response are only slightly higher, being 2.87 and 2.39 respectively. Therefore, it can be said with certainty that in reality multimedia teaching has a lot more room to be developed.

Table 13 Descriptive Statistics for Items III. 1-10

	Minimum	Maximum	Mean	Std. Deviation	Skewness
	Statistic	Statistic	Statistic	Statistic	Statistic
1. Much autonomy to students	2	5	3.57	.74	.021
2. Value individual difference	1	5	3.42	.78	-.610
3. Receive much feedback	2	5	3.59	.74	.119
4. I've used TPR	1	5	2.55	1.30	.201
5. I've used games	1	5	3.17	1.38	-.447
6. I've used the internet	1	5	2.59	1.38	.291
7. Used computer courseware	1	5	2.13	1.19	.878
8. Automatic habit is important	2	5	4.05	.76	-.565
9. Use of discipline					
10. I have various	2	5	3.78	.75	-.124
strategies	1	5	3.64	1.05	-.733

Another interesting finding is that participants responded quite positively to item 8 asking whether or not acquiring an automatic linguistic habit through repetition drills is important. Given this result, quite a number of respondents believe that Behaviorism or Audio-lingualism is no bad theory in teaching or learning English. This attitude of theirs is perhaps rooted in their own learning or teaching experience; otherwise, they would not have answered positively against their knowledge that either behavioristic psychology or the audio-lingual method of learning English based on it is apparently out of fashion. It is interesting to find out again their strong belief in behavioristic philosophy of education after it has been revealed in item II. 3.

In order to determine whether there is any significant difference in responding the above questions between pre-service and inservice sample population, the One-Way ANOVA test was also administered and the obtained F scores and probability levels are shown in Table 14.

As shown in the table, all the mean differences between preservice and inservice teachers are considered to be the results of random chance except for the two items: the fourth and fifth. The mean differences between preservice and in-service teachers in these items hold a statistical significance. Therefore, we will have to see how different their tallies are in the following Crosstabulation.

Regarding TPR experience and use of games, there is a conspicuous difference between preservice and inservice teachers in that the majority of the preservice students answered "absolutely not true." However, it is noteworthy that about half of the preservice students (23 of them) responded positively to the question if they have an experience in using games in the classroom. The high F value that these responses have is mainly

Table 14 One-Way ANOVA for Items III. 1-10

Items	Variable Type	df	Mean Square	F	Sig.
1. Much autonomy to students	Between Groups	1	.117	.212	.646
2. Value individual difference	Between Groups	1	2.255	3.788	.055
3. Receive much feedback	Between Groups	1	.300	.549	.461
4. I've used TPR	Between Groups	1	15.464	10.048	.002**
5. I've used games	Between Groups	1	12.644	7.070	.009**
6. I've used the Internet	Between Groups	1	5.151	2.766	.100
7. Used computer courseware	Between Groups	1	4.966	3.524	.064
8. Important automatic habit	Between Groups	1	.003	.006	.939
9. Use of discipline	Between Groups	1	1.783	3.255	.075
10. I have various strategies	Between Groups	1	3.905	3.632	.060

Table 15 Crosstabulation of Items III. 4 & 5

count

		4. TPR experience					Total
		absolutely not true	not true	so-so	true	absolutely true	
service	preservice	24	7	8	8	3	50
	inservice	3	10	10	13	2	38
Total		27	17	18	21	5	88

count

		5. use of games					Total
		absolutely not true	not true	so-so	true	absolutely true	
service	preservice	17	6	4	14	9	50
	inservice	1	4	8	21	4	38
Total		18	10	12	35	13	88

Table 16 Descriptive Statistics for Items III. 11-13

Items	Choices	Frequency	Percent	Skewness
11. Urgent need for a better teacher	• English proficiency • pedagogy • bridging generation gap • intensive English program • others	44 10 10 23 1	50.0 11.4 11.4 26.1 1.1	.500
12. Least proficient skill	• speaking • listening • reading • writing	35 23 6 24	39.8 26.1 6.8 27.3	.474
13. Type of teacher that I am	• diligent worker • power-wielder • service-provider • creative problem-solver • others	44 1 19 23 1	50.0 1.1 21.6 26.1 1.1	.268

due to the leftmost tally, that is, the "absolutely not true" slot. Other tallies do not vary greatly.

The skewness, frequencies, and percentages of the rest of the items in the third category are shown in Table 16. To the question "What would be the most urgent need of yours in making efforts to be a better English teacher?" Exactly half of the teachers picked "English proficiency." And to the question "Which is the least proficient area of yours?" the respondents indicated "speaking" or "writing" for their answer. Finally, to the question "What type of teacher do you suppose you are?" the answer choice "diligent worker" accounted for the half.

There were some differences found between the preservice and inservice teachers in responding to the last two questions while they were largely of the same opinion on the first item. The crosstabulation of Table 17 will tell us more about the last two items:

Half of the preservice teachers answered that the least proficient area of theirs lies in speaking whereas the area of listening has the most tallies in the case of the inservice teachers.

Table 17 Crosstabulation for Items III. 12 & 13

count

		12. least proficient area				Total
		speaking	listening	reading	writing	
service	preservice	25	10	2	13	50
	inservice	10	13	4	11	38
Total		35	23	6	24	88

count

		13. Type of teacher that I am					Total
		diligent worker	power-wielder	service provider	creative problem-solver	others	
service	preservice	19		12	18	1	50
	inservice	25	1	7	5		38
Total		44	1	19	23	1	88

Both groups picked "writing" as the second most difficult-to-learn area. As to the type of teacher, an overwhelming number of inservice teachers answered that they are diligent workers; on the other hand, the answers of the preservice teachers are split into the "diligent worker" and the "creative problem-solver." It is somewhat disappointing yet surprising that only 5 inservice teachers thought they were creative problem-solvers.

Toward the Item III. 11 asking what is the most urgent need for being a better English teacher, a high school teacher in Seoul answered: "Developing effective teaching and learning materials." To the question "What type of teacher do you suppose you are?" one preservice teacher answered "others," but did not specify the type.

To sum up, the respondents are not unwilling to give students autonomy, they rather value individual difference when they teach, and they receive a substantial amount of feedback. But they don't much make use of on-line information or a computer courseware and the preservice teachers are not much exposed to the TPR method. Even though they feel rather confident that they have various classroom strategies including collaborative learning, they are in favor of audio-lingual method of language learning. And they rather support the use of discipline in the classroom when delinquency occurs although they don't much believe in a power-wielder type of teacher. Based on the responses to multiple-choice items, both groups think that English proficiency is the most urgent need for better teaching, that speaking or writing is the least proficient skill area while the inservice teachers saw listening as the most problematic, and finally that they are among the diligent workers as a teacher. By and large, the respondents seem to prefer a rather traditional classroom where everything is properly controlled by the teacher but where innovation, either educational or formal, is a little hard to achieve.

3.3.4 Reflective Self-development

Under the fourth category, there are 10 Likert-type items which asked: 1) if you often reflect as a teacher on what you have taught how in the classroom; 2) if you have written a reflective journal after class; 3) if you have read an article written by a senior teacher or by your peer; 4) if you frequently utilize the Internet, visiting the web sites to find out the trend of other teachers and download the materials on line; 5) if you have talked about your teaching style with other teachers; 6) if you believe that critical reflection on your teaching behavior will help understand your teaching techniques; 7) if you have interest in the habit and way of thinking of your students as well as the new-generation movies and music in order to keep up with them; 8) if you believe that teacher development is to be done no less by conversation with colleagues than through personal experience; 9) if you enthusiastically join the in-service teacher training programs, workshops, and seminars; and 10) if you believe that teacher development is much influenced by the culture of your school.

As shown in Table 18, the participants responded rather positively to all of the questionnaire items, except for the second and third item.

Although there are 13 preservice teachers who did not answer, the 75 participants responded quite positively to the question "Do you reflect on your teaching as a teacher?" but they responded rather negatively to the question "Have you ever written a reflective journal?" with the mean score down to the "not true" level. All of the participants go on to confess that they do not have much experience in reading teacher stories. However, they seem to get more actively involved with other

Table 18 Descriptive Statistics for Items IV. 1-10

	N	Minimum	Maximum	Mean	Std. Deviation	Skewness
	Statistic	Statistic	Statistic	Statistic	Statistic	Statistic
1. Do you often reflect?	75	1	5	3.75	.89	-.549
2. Reflective journal experience	75	1	5	2.61	1.15	.482
3. Teacher stories	88	1	5	2.86	1.28	-.042
4. Visit web sites often	76	1	5	3.14	1.14	-.070
5. Talk with others about teaching	73	1	5	3.40	.89	-.402
6. Helpful critical reflection	88	2	5	3.81	.81	-.020
7. Understand student culture	77	2	5	3.99	.80	-.446
8. Collaborative development	88	2	5	4.00	.83	-.246
9. Enthusiasm for workshops	70	1	5	3.43	1.08	-.232
10. School influences TD.	78	2	5	4.04	.67	-.570

activities, as a diligent and dutiful teacher, such as frequently visiting Internet sites and talking with other colleagues about their teaching. No wonder most of them believe that critical reflection will help a teacher develop professionally. They also believe that collaborative work is important for teacher development and that the respondents are rather eager to join the workshops and seminars, as well as the inservice teacher training programs. To the question if they understand student culture, the respondents quite overwhelmingly said yes. And, to the question if they believe that teacher development is influenced by school culture, they also responded very positively.

In order to determine whether there is any significant difference in responding the above questions between preservice and inservice teachers, the One-Way ANOVA test was also administered and the obtained F scores and probability levels are presented in Table 19.

As shown in the table, as many as four mean differences between preservice and inservice teachers are considered to be statistically significant, not the results of random chance. Among these significant differences are the responses of Items 1, 7, 9 and 10. To determine the reasons for this phenomena, the crosstabulation for them was run as follows:

The first crosstabulation shows that the preservice teachers tend to be more reflective compared to the inservice teachers. This might be due to the fact that the teaching experience, whatever form it takes, of the preservice teachers is more novel and hence more vivid and powerful enough to stimulate them more to reflect whereas the teaching experience of the inservice teachers is more like a routine procedure as the sense of novelty wears off year in and year out. The second crosstabulation shows that both groups think they understand student culture

Table 19 One-Way ANOVA for Items IV. 1-10

Items	Variable Type	df	Mean Square	F	Sig.
1. Do you often reflect?	Between Groups	1	3.740	5.014	.028*
2. Reflective journal experience	Between Groups	1	.005	.004	.951
3. Experience in teacher stories	Between Groups	1	3.905	2.425	.123
4. Visit web sites often	Between Groups	1	1.592	1.230	.271
5. Talking with others	Between Groups	1	.921	1.156	.286
6. Helpful critical reflection	Between Groups	1	.020	.030	.863
7. Understand student culture	Between Groups	1	12.493	25.675	.000***
8. Collaborative development	Between Groups	1	.741	1.075	.303
9. Enthusiasm for workshops	Between Groups	1	9.306	8.809	.004**
10. School influences TD.	Between Groups	1	2.143	4.973	.029*

Table 20 Crosstabulation of Items IV. 1, 7, 9 & 10

count

		1. Do you often reflect?						Total
		absolutely not true	not true	so-so	true	absolutely true	no response	
service	preservice	1	2	4	20	10	13	50
	inservice		3	16	15	4		38
Total		1	5	20	35	14	13	88

count

		7. I understand student culture					Total
		not true	so-so	true	absolutely true	no response	
service	preservice		1	22	16	11	50
	inservice	3	15	15	5		38
Total		3	16	37	21	11	88

count

		9. enthusiasm for workshops						Total
		absolutely not true	not true	so-so	true	absolutely true	non applicable	
service	preservice	3	9	9	6	5	18	50
	inservice		1	15	14	8		38
Total		3	10	24	20	13	18	88

count

		10. School culture influences TD.					Total
		not true	so-so	true	absolutely true	no response	
service	preservice		3	26	11	10	50
	inservice	2	7	23	6		38
Total		2	10	49	17	10	88

fairly well, but the preservice teachers are of more conviction. The reason may be that the preservice teachers believe that they are younger and close to the life of the students they teach.

The third crosstabulation is related to the question if they enthusiastically join the inservice teacher training programs, workshops, and seminars. Therefore, there are 18 "no responses" tallies and the other responses of the preservice teachers are widely dispersed, which might indicate the various ways they interpret the question. For instance, the preservice teachers who have had an opportunity to attend a workshop or seminar probably answered "true" or "absolutely true." On the other hand, those who have had no such opportunity had no other way but answer "not true" or "absolutely not true." In other words, the responses of the preservice teachers should be interpreted with caution. However, this problem is no big matter or object of concern since the question is meant to target the inservice teachers. The attitude of inservice teachers seem to split here in that about half of them responded "so-so" or "not true" while about half of them responded "true" or "absolutely true."

The last crosstabulation gives a summary of the responses to the question if school culture influences teacher development. Both groups responded quite positively, but the preservice teachers seem more eager to say yes while the responses of the inservice teachers are more or less dispersed with a high negative skewness (The statistic is calculated as -.622). The intergroup difference of this question is probably due to the level of awareness that the actual reality of a school is not very different from that of another. The apparent high level of awareness might perhaps lead the inservice teachers to a dispersion of opinion which, in turn, might be said to represent the level of maturity of thought.

On the contrary, it is a high probability that the preservice teachers measured the influence of school culture on teacher development based on their memories of the schools they attended as a student. There is a remarkable difference in these two points of view. One is the insider's view as a teacher; the other is the outsider's view as a student. The teacher learns and after all comes to know the ins and outs of the job they practice; however, the student views the job only superficially, missing the essential nature of it. The latter, at most, sees the outside phenomena of the teacher, of teaching, and of the school culture. And, if he or she has an ear to the ground, the student will able to collect some hearsay. This may well be an over-interpretation. So, as for now, suffice it to say that there was an intergroup difference in responding to the school culture variable.

The skewness, frequencies, and percentages of the rest of the items in the fourth category are shown in Table 21. To the question "What is the most urgent need to improve the inservice

Table 21 Descriptive Statistics for Items IV. 11, 12 & 13

Items	Choices	Frequency	Percent	Skewness
11. Urgent need to improve inservice teacher education	• old facilities and fixtures	1	1.1	-.406
	• lack of systematic training	23	26.1	
	• lack of luring system	8	9.1	
	• lack of autonomy	2	2.3	
	• lack of overseas opportunity	8	9.1	
	• others	1	1.1	
	• no response	45	51.1	
12. Present method for reflection	• writing teaching journal	6	6.8	.738
	• sharing ideas with others	33	37.5	
	• preparing a portfolio	16	18.2	
	• success stories & episodes	9	10.2	
	• microteaching	3	3.4	
	• others	0	0	
	• no response	21	23.9	
13. Desirable method for reflection	• writing teaching journal	10	11.4	.649
	• sharing ideas with others	12	13.6	
	• preparing a portfolio	33	37.5	
	• success stories & episodes	9	10.2	
	• microteaching	8	9.1	
	• others	0	0	
	• no response	16	18.2	

teacher training programs?" The majority of the inservice teachers answered "lack of systematic training" while most of the preservice teachers showed no responses. And to the question "What do you do or have you done to be a reflective teacher?" the most respondents indicated "sharing ideas with others" for their answer. Finally, to the question "What would you rather do to be a reflective teacher?" the most answered response was "preparing a portfolio," followed by "sharing ideas with others," followed by "writing teaching journal."

There were some differences found between the preservice and inservice teachers in responding to the last two questions while the responses to the first question are mostly answered by the inservice teachers and most of the preservice teachers showed no response to it. The crosstabulation of Table 22 will tell us more about the responses to the last two items.

Table 22 Crosstabulation for Items IV. 12 & 13

count

		12. Present method for reflection						Total
		teacher journal	sharing ideas	portfolio preparation	collecting episodes	micro-teaching	no response	
service	preservice	5	11	7	4	2	21	50
	inservice	1	22	9	5	1		38
Total		6	33	16	9	3	21	88

count

		13. desirable method for reflection						Total
		teacher journal	sharing ideas	portfolio preparation	collecting episodes	micro-teaching	no response	
service	preservice	8	4	15	5	2	16	50
	inservice	2	8	18	4	6		38
Total		10	12	33	9	8	16	88

As shown in the first crosstabulation, the respondents, either from the preservice or the inservice group, reveal that "sharing ideas with others" is the way they reflect on their teaching. "Portfolio preparation" follows this idea and then follows the choice "teaching journal." There are 5 respondents among the preservice group declaring that they wrote teaching journal to reflect on their teaching; however, there is only one inservice teacher who made the same confession. This may be due to the overburdening effect of too much paper work poured on the shoulders of inservice teachers. It is only natural that they should avoid writing any more journal. Instead, they seem to prefer a much easier way of achieving reflection, that is, sharing ideas with their colleagues.

For a desirable method for reflection, an overwhelming number of respondents chose "portfolio preparation," which is followed by "teaching journal" in the preservice group and by "sharing ideas with others" in the inservice group who still avoid selecting "teaching journal." Writing teacher journal is a highly recommended method in the "reflection" literature. But, for some reason, there seems to be a strong rejection among the inservice teachers in Korea. They rather value microteaching for better reflection. There must be some reason for this, other than the one discussed above. One possible inference might be that the teaching journal, from the inservice teachers' point of view, is hard to write, time-consuming, and at best a game of words, but least helpful for any teacher to reflect because teaching needs spontaneity, quick wit or wisdom from long-time practice. It's not a kind of job that is to be improved by written reflection. If this is really so or not, we will find out in the following chapter.

Toward the Item 11 of Category IV asking what is the most urgent need to improve the inservice teacher education, a high school teacher in Seoul proposed: "that an extra budget for teachers to take courses at private institutes be appropriated while launching the credit bank system as soon as possible."

To sum up, most of the respondents seem to feel that they usually reflect on their teaching, but they seldom write a reflective journal. Moreover, they do not have much experience in reading teacher episodes. They get involved with other activities such as visiting Internet sites and talking with other colleagues about their teaching. They believe that critical reflection will be very helpful for their professional development, and that collaboration is also important for that purpose. The inservice teachers seem eager to participate in the workshops and seminars. They think they moderately understand student culture and they seem to believe that teacher development is more or less influenced by school culture even though there seems to be a slight difference in understanding this matter between the preservice and inservice teachers.

There are a few more differences found in the points of

view of the two groups: 1) the preservice teachers seem to be more reflective because they seem to be experiencing everything anew; 2) they also seem more convinced of the nature of student culture because they are younger and close to student life; 3) the preservice teachers' school experience is limited so they possibly misinterpret the questions according to their own understanding and hence the statistical analysis of their beliefs requires caution; and 4) compared to the preservice teachers, their maturer counterparts are less sure that school culture influences teacher development though their overall response is quite positive. This intergroup difference may be due to the level of awareness. Lastly, both groups are shown to reflect on their teaching mostly by "sharing ideas with others." But they believe that "portfolio preparation" is the best way to reflect on classroom teaching.

IV. DEVELOPING THE REFLECTIVE LANGUAGE TEACHING MODEL

4.1 Assumptions of Reflective Language Teaching

Reflective Language Teaching (RLT) goes for multiple perspectives to the problems of language teaching. It denies any affiliation to a particular method. It aims to find the best solution for a particular teacher to teach a particular lesson to a particular group of learners in a language classroom. Above all things, it draws on a recent trend in language teaching, that is, a movement away from methods and other external or top-down views of teaching toward an approach that seeks to understand teaching in its own terms.

Such an approach should start with the actual teaching processes, and seeks to gain a better understanding of these processes by exploring with teachers what they do and why they do it. As a matter of course, the result is the construction of an internal or bottom-up view of teaching. So, it is only natural that the nature of RLT be teacher-oriented, if not teacher-centered. It is to involve teachers planning their lesson, making decisions, and taking actions before collecting data about their own classrooms and their roles within them, and using that data as a basis for self-evaluation.

Such view of teaching is in no way new or innovative since it has been practiced from the very ancient times by eminent philosopher-teachers. But, as revealed in the Second Chapter, Deweyan tradition of regarding thinking as method and its continual emphasis on reflection and Schönian idea of "reflective practitioner" and its identification of reflection-in-action as the essence of expertise are the two main resources of Reflective Language Teaching. The other resources are from the inventory of the teacher beliefs and perceptions extracted from the survey research that has been discussed in the previous chapter. The researcher's years of language teaching experiences and philosophical intuitions are also the bases of the model development. Finally, the general assumptions and rationales for this conceptualization of English language teaching are as follows:

1. Teaching is a moral profession. A teacher's help could be a permanent influence on our entire life by giving us wings, so the role of a teacher was once equated with that of a king or of a parent in Korea. Unlike other practitioners, teachers demystify their own expertise and thus willingly abandon the source of power over the client that other professionals guard so jealously. Any teaching could be such a noble job.
2. Teaching is a craft profession. To be one, a teacher must acquire a sense of craft or a conscience of craft (Pratte and Rury, 1991, p. 131). And to develop continuously, a teacher goes through the stages of development. Reflective Language Teaching is a way of helping teachers to grow continuously, and especially, to go through the

initial stage of fear and confusion.

3. The proper province of Reflective Language Teaching draws on the ancient methodology of looking for solutions by utilizing the unique intellectual capacity of man. It rests on the belief that the human nature hardly changes despite the changes of times or of ages. The inquiring mind of a rational human being always looks for a solution when a problem arises, and RLT helps feed this universal capacity of man.
4. The nature of language and its acquisition is far more complex than anyone possibly thinks (Brown, 2000, p. 27). In order to teach students how to share and negotiate the meaning or conventions of English, teachers do well to implant an "empathy" skill. The "holistic" approach may take a firm stand in RLT in this respect.
5. Authenticity should be reinterpreted in that the "authentic" materials imported directly from English-spoken countries that hold linguistic hegemony should be our food for thought. A World English (WE) proponent, Kimberley Brown (In Hall & Hewings, 2001, pp. 108-117) bitterly criticizes on the Inner-Circle only perspective, contending that such a view promotes inequality and recommends that language education professionals work to create a resource bank of World Englishes for research and instruction.
6. Planning is of much importance. Unless there is a good planning, there is no good teaching. As Arita (1989) says, "A successful teaching is made up of 70% materials development and 30% dexterity" (p. 146). What to teach is no less important than how to teach. Planning also requires a great deal of teacher commitment; in this regard, the majority of the respondents of the survey

seem to have answered that the most important quality of a teacher is enthusiasm and commitment.

7. Many EFL teachers in Korea wish to take a trip to English-spoken countries. However, that is no guarantee of successful language teaching even if they have gotten a good look around the target country and thereby have had the necessary linguistic and cultural intake. If that is the way language teaching operates, the native speakers arriving back-packed will have to be the best teachers wherever they go.
8. As shown in the survey analysis, the philosophical tendency of English language teachers in Korea is something akin to eclecticism. They are not partial to any special methodology for their classroom action; they believe in the benefits of the Communicative Approach and at the same time they believe in the apparent strength of Behavioristic doctrines such as overlearning and repetition drill. This attitude of Korean English teachers toward eclecticism is well suited to the nature of reflective teaching.
9. RLT and CLT or other contemporary language teaching methods are not mutually exclusive. Rather, they share whatever strengths and merits they have. They are complementary in the sense that RLT needs to be a Korean version of CLT and that CLT is one of the most significant theoretical bases on which the 7th English Curriculum was molded.
10. Any approaches to good teaching in Korea must be concerned with the fact that teachers are already full-loaded with their tasks. RLT should not be such that it will be the straw that finally broke the camel's back. It should be such that the teachers will find a practical

value in it, that they will find it worthwhile for them to adopt this approach to English language teaching because it could save their time and make them successful.

4.2 The Three-Phase Cyclic Model

As stated, this study aims to provide a working model in order to promote critical reflection among the English language teachers in Korea. An essential first step in the development of reflective competence as a classroom English teacher is Planning, the thread that weaves the what of teaching with the how of teaching. In the case of teaching grammar, say, the third-person singular affixation, the decision making of how to teach, that is, the choice of inductive method and the preparation of the teaching materials such as the custom-tailored sentence inventory belong to this phase.

The Planning Phase, however, goes further because the classroom is a highly interactive and demanding place with a number of variables to be in control. Only planning thoroughly provides for some measure of order in an uncertain and changing environment. According to Freiberg & Driscoll (2000), research during the past 40 years on teaching effectiveness supports what most experienced teachers have concluded: effective teaching is not a haphazard process (p. 21). Expert teachers plan ahead to create an environment that is conducive for both their teaching style and student learning.

The second stage in the design process of RLT is Teaching, an act of taking actions to facilitate learning. By Widdowson's (1990) definition, teaching is "a self-conscious inquiring enterprise whereby classroom activities are referred to theoretical principles

. . . [which] . . . define the subject" (p. 1). On the other hand, Pratte & Rury (1991) ruminate that teaching is making relevant distinctions via some linguistic and logical skill. They also lay emphasis on a good command of the subject matter to enhance comprehension. According to Thornbury (2001), an EFL teacher's subject is defined within the realms of "language as a means to know the way the mind works" (p. 393). At the same time teachers must have a sense of their students to know which categories are likely to be sensible and meaningful to them.

Furthermore, the Teaching Phase entails the question of determining which modes of communication are most appropriate to the particular lesson and audience. Part of the decisions can be made in advance in the Planning Phase, but many of the decisions still have to be made in the classroom because teaching is a continuous quest to understand the students and "modulate to get in rhythm with them" (Joyce & Weil, 1996, p. 129). Thus every good language teaching entails learner-centered classrooms where learners are actively involved in their own learning processes (Nunan & Lamb, 2001. In Hall & Hewings, 2001, p. 27). However, it is also noteworthy that for some goals teacher-centered approaches to instruction are more effective (Eggen & Kauchak, 2001, p. 517).

The last phase of Reflective Language Teaching is Reflection, the path to deeper understanding of the instructional practice. A common teacher's understanding of classroom experience is rather synthetical than analytical and not rich or detailed enough to drive systematic reflection. So an intentional reflection is needed to empower the teacher to plan effectively and teach with easiness. In active reflection, teachers become empowered teachers who then turn into transformative intellectuals, intellectuals who are endowed with skills of critical reflectivity

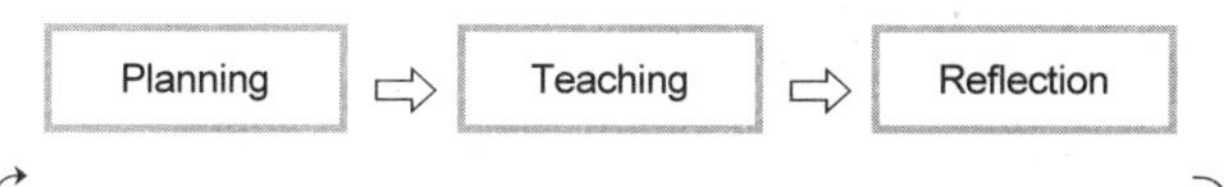

Figure 4 The Three-Phase Cyclic Model

and enlightened attitudes toward reform. In other words, critical reflection not only transforms a teacher's classroom but also has an impact on his or her school administration and on the society.

Reflection is meant to be active and militant toward the external forces as well as the internal mindset of an individual teacher. English education is also related to how we conceptualize teaching; thus, whether we view it as a set of neutral, value-free technical acts, or as a set of ethical, moral and political imperatives may well be important implications for the kind of reflective stance we adopt. So this is why we have to think about the macro linkage. An English teacher must not be "a cog in a self-perpetuating machine" as Tom warns (1985, p. 38).

As outlined above, the model for Reflective Language Teaching consists of three phases which are cyclic in nature in that if there is no good planning there is no good teaching; if there is no good reflection there is no good planning; and both good planing and good reflection will lead to good teaching. Everytime the circle operates, each phase feeds into the phase following immediately. Figure 4 and the recapitulating reminders that follow will summarize all this.

The specific features of each phase are as follows:

Phase One: Planning

The reflective language teachers:

- consider the feedback from the Reflection Phase

- decide on the main teaching point
- decide how to teach each teaching point
- find the best material for the topic of the lesson
- refer to the modern theoretical developments of language learning
- visualize what will kindle the students' interests
- decide on the key concepts to focus on
- decide on suitable learning activities
- anticipate the problem area
- anticipate the possible questions
- remember that language teaching is eclectic
- think about all possibilities from all perspectives
- carefully plan the productive use of time for instruction
- calculate the timing of each teaching stage
- bear in mind that no lesson works out exactly as planned
- pursue not simple rote-memory but deeper-level understanding
- think out some communicative contexts that will fit into the activities
- always analyze the learners' needs
- weigh the students' eye-level and arms' reach
- think about the possibilities of getting help from the community or from parents
- see to it that syllabus will include some of this: structures, notions and functions, themes and tasks, etc.
- set some macro-goals with aims or socio-cultural conditions of English education
- are a designer or a lesson-planner
- believe that a good lesson always feeds on hard work and a seeking mind

Phase Two: Teaching

The reflective language teachers:

- achieve proper set induction
- open up new areas of knowledge and practice
- consider that learners are tough, young and immature; unlock the doors with fun materials and enthusiasm in teaching
- care for each and every student of yours
- stand on the weaklings' side
- fumble around to finally find the right teaching persona
- succeed in emotional management and establish your own fiefdom
- raise the inquiring mind
- think of the constructivists' theory that good teaching does not necessarily guarantee good learning
- engage learners in expressing their own thoughts and feelings as often as possible
- calculate the interaction all the time
- use language data that is meaningful to the learner
- facilitate the communication process[1]
- at times step back and monitor the communicative process of learning
- make language learning meaning-based
- know that fluency entails accuracy; think about the error correction asking how much
- do the pairing and grouping as necessary in a smooth manner
- expect the temporal confusion in group activities
- onsider that EFL teaching should be "unbearably light"

---

[1] In CLT language learning is seen as a process that grows out of the interaction between learners, teachers, texts and activities (Breen & Candlin, 2001. In Hall & Hewings (Eds.), p. 14).

(Thornbury, 2001): in other words, English lesson should be fun, sucess-oriented and satisfying

- make the best of fun elements in the lesson
- develop and optimize a language pedagogy based on dialogue
- play skillfully by frequently crossing the linguistic and cultural border
- think of a code-switching method that could be nicely done in your classroom
- try teaching how to communicate as a member of international citizenship
- think out deconstructive ways of looking at target culture[2]
- control time systematically and carefully
- make the lesson lead the way to useful activities in later lessons
- remember that communicative evaluation emphasizes formative or ongoing evaluation, rather than summative or end-of-course evaluation

Phase Three: Reflection

The reflective language teachers:

- self-assess the lesson asking how well
- self-evaluate the lesson asking how effective
- pose and set the problems to address
- zero in on the most significant problem area that was discovered

---

[2] Deconstructive ways of looking at target culture imply asking "what if" questions such as: 1) What if you cut the bread with your knife and fork instead of breaking it with hands? 2) What if you make noise when you eat tomato soup? 3) What if you drink milk while chewing the bread? or 4) What if you eat the stake left-over for your breakfast? and so on. Such questions may or may not have correct answers. The main thing is that the learners have chances to imagine being in other people's shoes.

- consider the ways to help out the low achievers
- examine the strengths and weaknesses of the technique used
- find a way to avoid mannerism or routinized practice
- amass self-knowledge by asking: Who am I in the lives of these kids?
- remember that teaching does not exist in isolation from the content, the students' background and the surrounding world
- consider the ways to become more flexible, sensible and appropriate
- think about the type of teacher that I am: 1) self-referencing; 2) ego-enhancing; 3) self-effacing (Ellwein et al., 1989)
- reflect on successful areas of lesson
- reflect on unsuccessful areas of lesson
- remember that reflection is a teacher-oriented theorizing and could influence future research and policy making
- ask: what stage is my reflection on among the technical, practical, and critical reflection? (Van Manen, 1977)
- look for an opportunity to talk to others about teaching
- reflect on value conflicts when your values cannot guide your actions and thus hinder you from performing the roles of teacher
- check your reflection based on the following forms of action: 1) describe: what do I do? 2) inform: what does this mean? 3) confront: how did I come to be like this? and 4) reconstruct: how might I do this differently? (Smyth, 1989)
- think about the extent of revision
- revise the plan for the next lesson
- look back on your teaching with some macro-goals

As we have seen so far, the act of teaching in the mode

of Reflective Language Teaching is made up of three modules each of which runs separately with a tendency to feed into the next module. Hence the tripartite model is operated cyclically and in its ultimate process the accumulated cycles develop spirally into each upgraded stage of skills development.

Let's think of an appropriate instance here, where a middle school English teacher, Mrs. Kim, notices her students frequently making mistakes when dealing with the third-person singular present tense sentences in their diary writing. Even though she has made a couple of comments on this, the students seem to need some other treatments. She decides that this particular grammatical point be taught inductively in the next class session. She thinks over and over again as to the best fit data, and finally comes up with a decent inventory. She brings the sentences to her class and first asks students to categorize the data into two groups: sentences with V and sentences with V-(e)s. She then asks them to think about the conditions the second group of sentences have. The students find out the grammatical differences in person, number and tense. They finally understand why some of the sentences need a verb form ending *-s* or *-es*.

4.3 Putting Together Micro- and Macro-Reflection

The RLT model described above has dealt with the micro-level classroom teaching. All the efforts converge on a classroom English teacher's fumbling around for a way to establish a powerful emotional and intellectual link with students that is effective and sustainable. The teachers also look for the "teaching persona" that works best for them (Labaree, 2000,

p. 230). This persona is both natural and constructed by the will of the teacher, and enables people with remarkably different personalities to come out good teachers, who, as an underlying thread, ought to share such qualities as openness, responsiveness, flexibility, or evenhandedness (Maxwell & Meiser, 2001, p. 440).

On the other hand, the teacher as a reflective practitioner should base his or her teaching on the knowledge base, or in Schön's (1987) terminology, on the "appreciation system", that is, the domains of scholarship and experience. This knowledge base or the "appreciation system" consists of two major parts: one is concerned with classroom and the learners while the other reaches out up to school and society (Shulman, 1987).

Teaching is basically a social profession. In addition to dealing with what takes place in the classroom, it should address the problems of bigger circles, namely, school and society. It is also imperative that teachers put on their reflective agenda the macro concerns about political and ethical principles underlying classroom teaching and confront the knowledge/power issue in order to be truly reflective. For, according to Smyth, "reflection without action is verbalism; action without reflection is activism" (1989, p. 5). Reflection could thus be equated to educational reform.

A stronger version of Reflective Language Teaching, therefore, does not stop at the improved teaching in an individual classroom. It dashes out and mouths its idea in public, collectively finding out the best possible solutions to the current educational problems. Without a spirit of militant reflection, either correcting the erroneous stipulations or closing the gap between policy and practice cannot possibly be achieved. Now, the three-phase RLT model is to be expanded to involve Macro factors as shown in Figure 5.

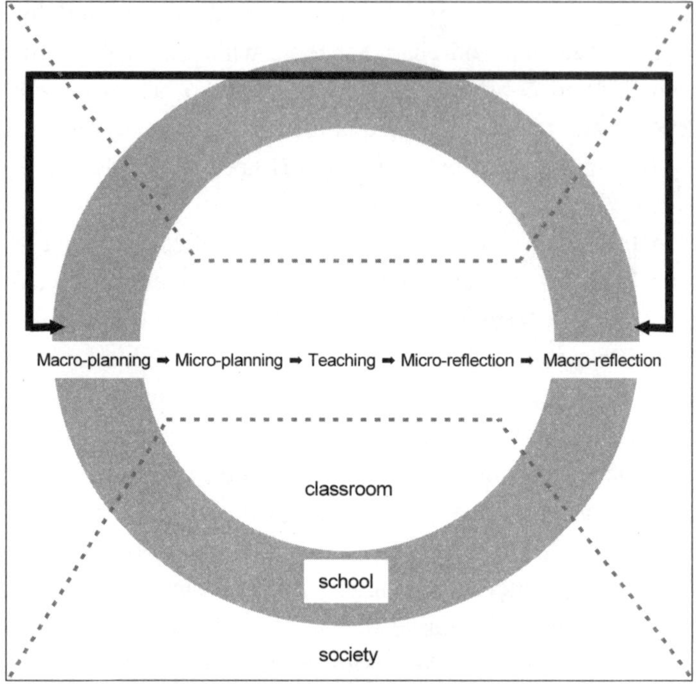

Figure 5 The Expanded RLT Model

In the diagram, the two ellipses and the outer rectangle represent the enlarging spheres of reflection: classroom, school and society, respectively. The two dotted lines, which converge at first and run parallel with each other before diverging at last, symbolize the varying scope of teacher reflection. Finally, the arrows represent the flow of reflective process. In this five-phase model each phase feeds its way into the next phase; hence, the operation is both linear and cyclical. However, one difference from the three-phase model is that this model has two alternative cycles. The first cycle which is related to the smaller ellipse starts with micro-planning and then moves on to the teaching phase that moves on to the micro-reflection

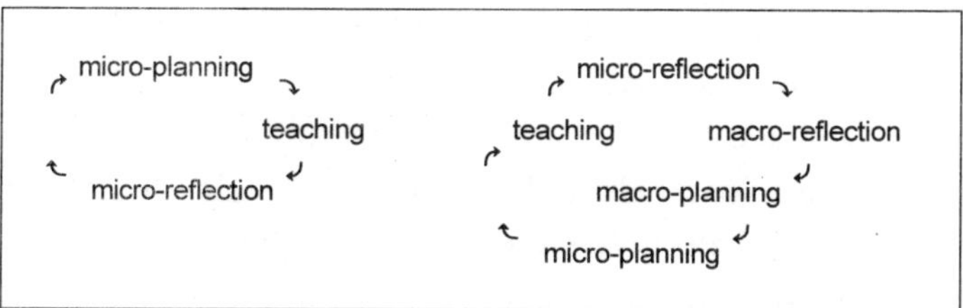

Figure 6 The Two RLT Cycles

phase, and finally returns to the micro-planning phase, which is exactly the same process as we have seen in the three-phase model. The second cycle which compasses the larger elliptical area starts with micro-reflection which moves on to macro-reflection, and then to macro-planning, and then to the final teaching phase. This twofold cyclic operation can be diagramed in the following schemata.

In this combinative model, the five phases of Reflective Language Teaching finally develop into seven phases which constitute one full cycle: 1) micro-planning; 2) teaching; 3) micro-reflection (These phases are due to the smaller ellipsis denoting 'classroom.'); 4) macro-reflection (From this phase the operation moves to the right cycle.); 5) macro-planning (These two phases are due to the larger ellipsis denoting 'school.'); 6) micro-planning; and 7) teaching (Notice the phases are entering the smaller ellipsis again).

There are two recurrent stages of micro-planning and of teaching; other phases occur only once. At a glance, the resulting cycle the starting node of which is "micro-planning" seems contradictory to the expanded RLT model which starts with "macro-planning." But one should note that since the overall operation is cyclical, every node can be a starting node. So, as in this case, "micro-planning" may well be a starting node.

Now, let's discuss each phase of the full RLT cycle in some

detail. Micro-planning is a stage where what to teach and how to teach it in the particular English classroom are decided. Foreign language teaching involves making a good number of individual decisions before the action in the classroom. These small decisions help a foreign language teacher to coast along on the prefabricated lesson plan. Though any effective teaching necessitates a thorough planning, foreign language teaching including ELT especially could use the gift of foresight. If it is a really impressive lesson and thus makes students feel empowered to communicate in some way, more than half of the language lesson has to be visualized in advance in the teacher's mind. In other words, most of the content to be delivered must be chewed and digested in the teacher's imagination before being actually served later in the classroom.

The content or the input does not matter very much whether it is comprehensible or incomprehensible, since the teacher who is intellectually alive enough can tell immediately whether it is teachable or not. For, an effective language teacher never leaves the interzone, once called Zone of Proximal Development (ZPD) by Vygotsky. It is the territory where language teachers live and work. One more reason why a previously relived experience of lesson planning is essential for foreign language teaching is that in doing so the modelling of the teacher in the classroom will be more spontaneous and more able to show any closeness to authenticity. To put it another way, the more mentally exercised the lesson is the better modelled and successfully presented it will be in the classroom.

Propelled by the first phase comes the second phase Teaching. Proper set induction is important in any type of teaching; however, achieving proper set induction is not enough. For a really effective language lesson, the game of winning the young minds in the classroom must be done within no more than five minutes. Telling a couple of hackneyed jokes or making a fool of some hapless individual to force the rest of the class into a laugh will hardly be a good way of opening up. A blitz of fresh content-related ideas that will ignite the young hearts at once is to be sought and presented at some moment that could catch them off guard. A good language teacher is a bit of the magician changing the scarf into a dove at some unexpected moment, waving his or her magic wand.

The second reminder is that language development is a cumulative process, not produced by one specifically identifiable event, but rather by the cumulative effect of a number of events. According to Van Lier, the development goes through three processes: acquisition, retention, and extension (1988, p. 92). Acquisition here means the knowledge or skills 'taken in' and it must be retained over time and extended through application in varied relevant work. So the interaction plays an important role; it mediates between "input" and "intake" and consists of social interaction, ie., interaction with others and cognitive interaction, ie., interaction with existing knowledge systems (Ibid., p. 93). Classroom teaching is a job that handles these variables. Lastly, a good language teaching uses time systematically and productively. In the form of appropriate closure, it makes the lesson lead the way to useful activities in later lessons so that class goes on.

In the phase of Micro-reflection, the two most important virtues are open-mindedness and responsibility. To properly reflect on what we have done in the classroom, we first have to be honest about our ability and capacity to the extent that we may confess to our ignorance and occasional inconsiderateness. This does not mean, however, that we have to blame or punish ourselves for every fault or failure to learn that takes place in the classroom. It only refers to the fact that when we sufficiently open up our mind we can notice the problem areas in our teaching. Otherwise, there will be no inquiring mind nor a critical reflection whatsoever.

The responsible attitude toward our profession is also crucial. Without the eagerness to do a fine job or the enthusiasm to create some changes among the learners, the teacher will not be able to bear the extra burden of reflecting on what he or she has already done to guide them to learning. Micro-reflection is a way of looking for better choices when the teacher hits the "forked road." It involves the ability to make rational choices with both "received knowledge" which is the necessary intellectual content of the profession and previous "experiential knowledge" which has been developed by practice of the profession (Wallace, 1991, p. 15). In that sense teaching is a most learned profession. Chances are that the more you know, the better you will be able to teach and the better you will be able to reflect.

Macro-reflection concerns the troubling mind as well as the critical mind. As Schön (1983) so aptly put it, "The situations of practice are not problems to be solved but problematic situations characterized by uncertainty, disorder and indeterminacy" (pp. 15-16). Practitioners are therefore engulfed in wrangles over conflicting and competing values and purposes. Let's take for an example the case of adopting an EFL teaching approach. While not all teachers see themselves as trying to implement a particular approach or methodology (e.g., Grammar-Translation Method, Communicative Language Teaching, a Whole Language Approach, the Direct Method, Active Teaching, Audiolingualism, Total Physical Response), many teachers do describe their teaching in these terms and have actually been trained to work within a specific methodology.

For instance, a more recent model of teaching, Active Teaching is used in mainstream education in Western countries (Richards & Lockhart, 1994, p. 102). It focuses on the teacher's ability to engage students productively on learning tasks during lessons and sees the management and monitoring of learning as a primary role for teachers. On the other hand, the over-a-century-old Direct Method proposes the following guidelines:

> Never translate: demonstrate
> Never explain: act
> Never make a speech: ask questions
> Never imitate mistakes: correct
> Never speak with single words: use sentences
> Never speak too much: make students speak much
> Never use the book: use your lesson plan
> Never jump around: follow your lesson plan
> Never go too fast: keep the pace of the students
> Never speak too slowly: speak normally
> Never speak too quickly: speak normally
> Never speak too loudly: speak normally
> Never be impatient: take it easy
>
> (Titone, 1968, pp. 100-101)

Absurd as it may sound, the "natural" way of language teaching enjoyed considerable popularity through the end of the nineteenth century and well into the twentieth. It was most widely accepted in private language schools where students were highly motivated and where native-speaking teachers could be employed (Brown, 2000, p. 45). Indeed, it could still be a good approach to language teaching only if the few preconditions are met or only if a few items are discarded. The important thing is, whatever approach or method we believe in or try to implement, that the undeniable fact remains: a method is the product of the particular space and time. As a macro-reflector, an EFL teacher must consider this aspect of all methodologies in fashion. The methodological fads come and go; none of them are here to stay forever.

More expanded scope of Macro-reflection lies in the two most important institutional factors: school and society. More often than not, these two institutions impede or at least fail to support micro-level teaching as in Ahn's (2000) case. However, as the survey research has suggested in the previous chapter, it is believed that teacher development is more or less influenced by school culture. The school climate or "ethos" is then influenced by the society. They are interrelated variables to teachers and teaching. According to Weldon (1971), educational systems are designed to serve the needs of the culture in a particular society. In American society, as he describes, there are five cultures competing for general acceptance.

First, 'perennialists' are regressivists who would go back to the eternal truths or "Great Ideas" of classical culture and would inculcate these specially privileged truths into students' outlooks. Second, 'essentialists' are conservatives who would preserve, conserve, and transmit the essential, enduring truths of American heritage through indoctrination. Third, 'exitentialists' are individualists who are striving to achieve a culture based on individual freedom. They believe that schools should foster student freedom and self-direction. Fourth, 'reconstructionists' are radicals who believe that a cultural upheaval, fostered through indoctrination of collectivism, will inevitably usher in a socialistic, future-centered, "new social order." Lastly, 'pragmatists' foster reflective thinking. They would set up, perpetuate, and change cultural institutions on the basis of reflective study of the suitability of such institutions (Ibid., p. 1).

In Korean society as well, all five of these cultures can be found. It is also true that they are bidding against each other to take the educational hegemony. Some educators who could be categorized into either 'perennialists' or 'essentialists' try hard to maintain their conservative stance. Others believe in so-called "alternative schooling" where the students, usually surrounded by a natural environment, are made to learn by experience in a very slow pace without being pushed to achieve as in other normal schools. They must be 'existentialists'. There are still others who participated in the "true education" movement a decade ago and who are of the National Teachers Union. They could be called 'reconstructionists.'

Needless to say, reflective educators are 'pragmatists'. They try to transform the school and the society they are in on the basis of reflective study. Prior to reflective study, they would not insist that any particular cultural patterns should be either accepted or rejected. As in the case of adopting a suitable language teaching method, they defer their decision, insisting that all institutional patterns, especially the top-down schemata be subjected to criticism and appraisal. Eventually, a reflective teacher's role is to take a critical look at the interactive relationship between schools and society.

Macro-planning, the fifth phase, is fed with the awareness of the macro concerns arising from Macro-reflection. First of all, it concerns itself with aims of education, curriculum and method. A middle school English teacher should think about the aims of middle school English education which are manifested in the 7th English Curriculum; that is, 1) to develop the learners' communicative competence so as to be prepared for the upcoming age of internalization and globalization; 2) to help students have interest in and affinity for English; and 3) to enhance their level of understanding of foreigners and of their cultures. Middle school English curriculum is developed to achieve these educational aims, and it is best embodied in the endorsed textbooks that are adopted and used by English teachers at local schools. The textbooks are organized in the form of notional-functional syllabus and heavily draw on the Communicative Approach. So, at a glance, there seems to be little choice left for the on-site English teacher but to adopt the CLT approach.

The roles of a language teacher who adopts the methodology of CLT may prove too much for a local English teacher; then he or she can compromise and negotiate after a thorough Macro-reflection on the matter. Then, in the Macro-planning stage, the teacher may design his or her own version of CLT that is fitted into the ability of the teacher and the students. This compromise or negotiation or renegotiation will not necessarily lessen the quality of language teaching and/or learning. Rather, it may empower the teacher and the learners to enjoy their English lesson and thus to develop their communicative competence and their understanding of foreigners and of their culture.

The fifth phase in turn feeds its way into the sixth and seventh phase, respectively, micro-planning and teaching which constitute the second turn of the first and second phase. This second time around of the micro-planning and teaching phases, however, will be more than slightly different from the first time since this cycle is loaded with the input from the fourth and fifth phase, namely, Macro-reflection and Macro-planning. The second cycle of micro-planning and teaching will thus turn out as rich and powerful as the amount of input taken in. In this way the teachers who engage in this method of reflective planning and teaching will get empowered step by step and get spirally developed with the cyclical operations going on and on.

So far mainly the structural aspects of Reflective Language Teaching have been discussed. If the proposed model is not to be degenerated into another vague and barren theorization, however, a specific example of implementing this model to classroom language teaching will have to be presented to strike any balance. So the author will take for an example another case of teaching English to Middle School first graders. Suppose you have spent two-thirds of the first semester and you are now covering Lesson 5 of the adopted textbook published by Didimdol in 2000. As the title of the lesson "Can you send some gimbap over the Internet?" will suggest, this lesson is mostly about e-mail correspondence between a Korean student and her American counterpart. The communicative syllabus of this lesson tells us that we should teach three functions in this lesson: requesting, asking about remembering, and answering about remembering focusing on such expressions as "Do you remember your last field trip?" and "Yes, I remember it well."

This lesson is supposed to be finished within two weeks. Mrs. Kim, our imaginary teacher, is at her desk in the teachers' office. Yesterday she finished the last portion of Lesson 4. She is now planning on what she will do with Lesson 5 in today's class. Thus begins the first phase of the RLT cycle:

Phase One: Micro-planning

- Today I will cover the first portion of Lesson 5: Warm Up, Listen & Check and Listen & Act. This is the listening portion of the lesson.
- In the Warm Up exercise, I will focus on the communicative functions specified by the modal verbs *can*, *do*, and *please*.

- I will make sure how much the students understand the content of the taped material.
- The students will listen to Listen & Check and Listen & Act twice with some interval. In the interval give explanation to some crucial points or to difficult language forms, and then get them to listen for the second time.
- Check the individual level of understanding randomly during the exercises.

Now she goes to teach her class. Thus begins the second phase:

Phase Two: Teaching

- The introduction to the new lesson is adequate. I ask to the students, "how was the last school trip to Railroad Museum?" Many answer, "It was fun."
- Before getting into the main listening, I urge the students to pay good attention following the rhythm of the spoken utterances. I give two reasons for this: first, we should process information as fast as we can to understand most of the message; second, we should not let the unnecessary thinking intercept our concentration while listening.
- From time to time I ask students how much they are understanding the portion they have just heard.
- Even after repeated listening, some students are still missing the important part of the message. So I go over the portion one more time.

Soon Mrs. Kim finishes her teaching and goes back to the teachers' office. She reflects on her teaching:

Phase Three: Micro-reflection

- On second thought, students seem to have difficulty

listening to the past forms of verb such as *sang*, *wrote*, or *went*. Even if they hear the sounds of these verb forms, the students either fail to understand what they signifie or cannot instantly distinguish them from their present-tense forms. This is the area that requires a special treatment. Maybe more form-focused exercises will be necessary.
- Students' speed of processing sound input is rather slow. They tend to listen word by word in a top-down manner. I might have to teach them one day how to spread the net using their pre-knowledge, ie., their schemata when they listen.

Now she reflects on macro factors:

Phase Four: Macro-reflection

- The possible problem while teaching this unit will arise from the letter-writing exercise. The students may have a strong desire to express something to their counterpart, but chances are they don't know yet how to write or what to write. Teaching the first graders how to write a letter or what to write is no easy job. Either I may skip it this time or I may tackle this spending a couple of extra hours.
- But, in view of the goal of teaching Middle School English I, the problem of teaching English for real communication still remains even after I have taught the students the skill of letter-writing. How shall I handle this problem?
- The best way is to provide a good communicative context where the students use the target language for real communication. One good idea is to find a classroom in a foreign country that has a similar need for English pen pals.

She sets the problem seeking macro solutions:

Phase Five: Macro-planning

- Our school has a sisterhood relationship with a middle school in Fukuoka, Japan. How about asking out the English teachers there to get our students connected?
- In order to discuss the matter with other teachers and get other necessary helps, I will see the Principal today. As soon as the outline of the project is drawn up, we should do our best to launch it fast and accurate. An intramural committee may have to be formed for this purpose. And the promotion activity of making it known to the students and parents will have to get started sooner rather than later to get the most help possible.
- The English teachers in our school may have to share the material that effectively deals with the themes of letter-writing and self-introduction. I will talk about this matter with the senior teacher.

She now plans on what she will do in the next classroom:

Phase Six: Micro-planning

- First of all I will tell the students what project we are up to. And then I will ask them to decide on the name of the project. We may call it Project X. I will tell them the success of Project X depends on their active participation.
- The main part of the job on the students' side is to write a decent letter properly introducing themselves.
- They have to know every word in their letter really matters so that the overall tone of their letter sounds polite.

Now she goes to class again with a new-found desire to

teach better as she wants to be a big help to students who are supposed to correspond with foreign students in a week or so. Thus begins the last phase of the 7-step Reflective Language Teaching:

Phase Seven: Teaching

- Students are glad to participate in Project X. They seem sure that this will be a lot of fun as well as being enlightening.
- Students learn better because they really want to write better letters to their counterparts. The educational context, though artificial, provides the students with a chance for real communication, which makes it possible for them to have an intrinsic motivation for studying English.
- I teach the basic elements of an ordinary letter including heading, salutation, body, complimentary close, and signature.
- I teach them how to sound polite in writing letters in English.
- Whatever I teach them today, the students never cease to show maximum concentration. I feel like an awesomely good teacher.

This is the brief summary of the imaginary process where Reflective Language Teaching is run stage by stage in its specific implementation level. The bottom line is that the overall operation is both cyclical and spiral. Each stage feeds its way into the next and finally develops into an organic whole. In the structure of the RLT model all the variables of language teaching including the three steps and the micro and macro factors are interdependent and gyrate together to reach the best solution to the perceived problems of foreign language teaching.

V. THE APPLICATION OF THE RLT MODEL

5.1 Activating the Planning Phase to Develop RLT Syllabus

As revealed in the findings of the survey research, both the preservice and inservice English language teachers in Korea seem to believe that teaching can be a pleasurable job but that it demands a lot of commitment and hard work for success. They also appear to believe that they have to grow steadily in order not to lag behind the times of change. One important problem is that the majority of them hold a belief that English proficiency is the most urgent need for better teaching. As mentioned earlier, however, this could be misleading in that the teachers might direct most of their efforts toward improving their own proficiency, which might result in the negligence of the teaching itself.

From a reflective language teacher's point of view, the successful teaching of English does not lie in improving one's own English proficiency but in concentrating on the teaching itself. As to the question "What is teaching?" the tenet of

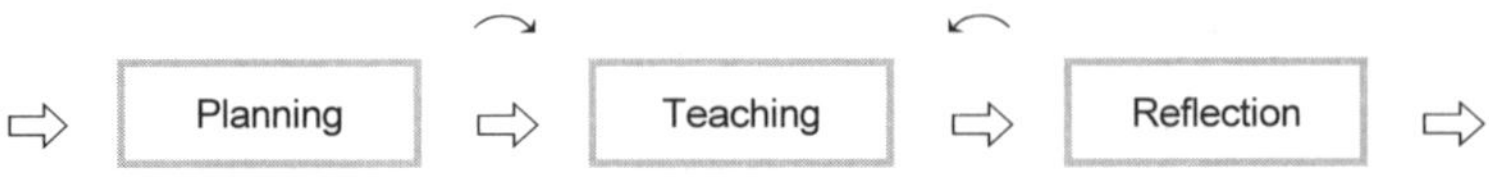

Figure 7 The Two-Way Input System

Reflective Language Teaching relates to a good viable definition of teaching. According to the theorists of reflective teaching, teaching is 'inquiry' that leads to problem-setting and problem-solving. It is a practical, bottom-up way of craft acquisition, and above all things it implies an aesthetic sense for style. As Whitehead (1967) elucidates, 'style' is "the last acquirement of the educated mind." It is also referred to as "the most useful." English language teachers in Korea should outgrow the prevalent myth that English proficiency will be a panacea for all the problems of teaching. The teachers with improved ability in English speaking will perhaps gain back their self-esteem, but regaining self-esteem alone does not make them go afar.

As already discussed in the previous chapter, the proposed model for Reflective Language Teaching is composed of three interrelated modules: Planning, Teaching, and Reflection. It was suggested that the operation of the model be cyclic because each module has to be fed into one another. If the focus is to be laid on the phase of Teaching, however, it could be that Teaching receives input from both sides, that is, from Planning and Reflection. Figure 7 will show how this operation works.

In this schema, as the arrows on the top indicate, Planning is to serve Teaching. Reflection is also destined to serve Teaching after it serves Planning first. Therefore, quality input from both Planning and Reflection is crucial for successful teaching. So, in order to ensure good teaching, the phases of Planning and Reflection should be activated to the full. In other words, in order to activate the phase of Teaching, the two other phases should be activated first.

This chapter will concern the ways to activate the Planning Phase before finding out the best ways to implement the Reflection Phase. First of all, to activate the Planning Phase is to set problems. Effective planners are those who ask proper questions. With an inquiring mind developed and refined in reflective practices, they are likely to ask the following questions if they are supposed to teach English successfully to grade school students:

(1) How can I help the students to reach deeper understanding of English?
(2) What should be authentic English for my students?
(3) What are appropriate communicative contexts for my students?
(4) Should I teach grammar separately? If so, how can I do so most effectively?
(5) How can I help the students to achieve the twofold goal, fluency and accuracy?

By no means is this list meant to be exhaustive. There could be far more questions or problems to address in classroom English teaching. But this will be sufficient to show the crucial problem areas. Any good teaching and/or planning will probably have to deal with these problems.

Secondly, to activate the Planning Phase is to consider both macro and micro factors of RLT in a balanced way. Macro factors including educational aims, curriculum, syllabus, teaching methods, and milieu such as school and society are usually predetermined. It is evident that English language teachers must function within a national curriculum framework. So, they have to diligently accustom themselves to those external factors so as not to let any of them impede their planning or teaching.

However, several times more attention should be given to micro factors of planning such as activity plans, floor plans, teaching aids, fun materials, multimedia equipment, classroom management and so on. By the way, most of the above mentioned reflection questions are more related to micro factors than to macro factors. Therefore, the job of an individual teacher is mostly Micro-Planning while the job of a policy elite is to tackle Macro-Planning.

Finally, to activate the Planning Phase is to develop proper units of instruction. At classroom level it means to come up with a good lesson plan. Planning is nothing less than converting the content knowledge on the textbook into a form of pedagogical content knowledge that will be effectively used in the classroom. RLT lesson plans must contain this 'pedagogical content knowledge,' that special "amalgam of content and pedagogy" which is "uniquely the province of teachers" (Shulman, 1987, p. 8). A properly made lesson plan of a reflective teacher will thus consist of such guidelines of teaching as unit objectives, methods or techniques to be used, main teaching points, some do's and dont's, 'authentic' data, anticipated problem areas, time allotment, extemporaneous tactics, feedback techniques, reinforcement tactics, communicative activities, structural portions for giving explanation, structural and/or colloquial portions for audio-lingual practice, and so forth.

Now, let's think about designing a sample syllabus. The target students are Middle School first graders, and the textbook being used here is *Middle School English I* published by Doosan in 2000, one of the 13 textbooks the use of which has been authorized by the Ministry of Education. The syllabus will be described mainly in expository style with the macro and micro factors introduced in a numerical order.

1. General Aims: In the 7th Curriculum, the threefold goal of English teaching is described as efforts 1) "to develop the learners' communicative competence so as to be prepared for the upcoming age of internalization and globalization, 2) to help students have interest in and affinity for English, and 3) to enhance their level of understanding of foreigners and of their cultures" (Development Committee, 1997, p. 17). (Author's translation) Teachers only have to follow this guideline when they plan on their individual lesson.
2. Curriculum: The 5 key elements in the New Curriculum include the following.

   ① The English curriculum has a required subject and an elective subject. The former applies to the third grade of Elementary School through to the first grade of High School. The latter applies to the second and third grades of High School.

   ② A proficiency-based language program is introduced. It allows students to learn according to their own abilities and interests.

   ③ The 7th Curriculum has reduced the contents of learning by 30% over the 6th Curriculum. These changes were reflected in textbooks so the volume of the textbooks were reduced and the contents became easier.

   ④ The New Curriculum intends to foster accuracy and fluency by presenting communicative functions and example sentences.

   ⑤ Diverse teaching techniques can be used. They may include Total Physical Responses, Silent Way, Suggestopedia, Audio-Lingual Method, Community Language Learning, Communicative Approach, Whole Language Approach.
3. Methods: Most of the teaching methods recommended by the New Curriculum are linked to cognitive approach. Grammar-Translation Method and Audio-Lingual Method

based on Behavioristic Psychology and Structuralism are relegated to an out-of-date methodology. Reflective language teachers, however, will not discard any of these methods since the asserted doctrine of RLT is eclectic. If a method is appropriate for the given content and for the given learners, the teachers need never be shy of adopting it. The main goal is to help the learners achieve deeper understanding of the content so as to make it easy for them to understand, parse, and retrieve better in the future.

4. School and Society: The newly arrived teacher should know the local school culture upon which his or her professional development might depend. In most of the cases, today's schools are afflicted with a high degree of competition. Reflective language teachers should do well to make the best of this situation without letting the competitive culture get the best of them. In other words, competition needs to be used as a facilitating factor, forbidden to be a debilitative element. Teachers should always be alert to the needs of society. They must keep up with the change of the times. To do all these duties successfully, the teachers who are in charge of the same subject, English in this case, need to get together on a regular basis. In the meetings the principal often needs to be present to support and coordinate the problem-solving or decision-making.
5. Parents: Reflective language teachers should think of parents as important partners. They should lead the parents to understand that on this stage getting their sons and daughters involved in learning English is the most significant of all. They ought to be let known that getting interested in English and approaching it in a variety of ways is much more important than studying overnight for the coming exam and getting good marks on it. Trust is also important in the relationship of teachers to parents. Teachers should not

beafraid of showing their care and enthusiasm toward the students and have to make sure that the parents know the efforts of the teachers. In doing so, they may be able to have the parents support the teaching. If a conflict arises, the two parties concerned convene to bridge the gap.

6. One Academic-Year Syllabus: For Middle School first graders, the one academic year consists of two semesters, Spring and Fall. One semester is made up of 20 weeks. But, one week is typically spent for school functions. And there are also holidays. The actual time allotted for class sessions usually amounts to 18 weeks. There are about 4 English classes a week; therefore, there are 76 hours in total allotted for one semester. Table 23 will show the content and pedagogy to be used for the whole year of teaching. The first semester covers up to Lesson 6, and the total amount of time allotted is 60 hours. The rest of the hours are for reviews, for exams, for more skill-oriented exercises, or for field trips. (In the table, the capital letter T and L in the first and second slot stand for "Theme" and "Lesson," respectively.)
7. A Sample Unit[1] and Lesson Plan: On the surface, drawing up a lesson plan seems simple: specify objectives, design learning activities to help students reach them, and assess the extent to which the objectives have been reached. However, it isn't as simple as it appears on the surface because it requires extensive content knowledge and clear pedagogical thinking. It would be no exaggeration to say

[1] The term "unit" was used here to refer to that which is more flexible than "lesson." According to Maxwell and Meiser (2001), a "unit" is an organized block of instruction; it includes goals for the course of study, the materials the teacher and students will use, activities, the sequence of instruction, and ways student learning will be evaluated. Unlike a lesson, a unit varies in length, anywhere from a few days to weeks, depending on the content. It is something that teachers create. Within it, daily lesson plans are also developed, which as a shorthand version may not be elaborate.

that instruction consists of 70% planning and 30% teaching. Good planning mostly guarantees good teaching. Here, among the 12 lessons, Lesson 7 has been chosen for the sample unit. This is the starting lesson for the second semester. As they have had the first semester, the students now understand fairly well how the usual lesson proceeds. The procedure is described in a simple format.

The first period of the 7th unit which is made up of 10 periods has been picked for a sample lesson. Meanwhile, the sample unit is described on the Master Plan in Table 24, and the sample lesson is described on the Sub-plan in Table 25.

Table 23 One-Year Syllabus for Middle School English I

T	L	Title	Content/Objectives	Context/Activities	Time
My World	1	My Friend Cyber Bob	• Expressions for introduction • Forms of *be*	• Students ringfamily photo • Introduce family	9 hours
	2	My Favorite Pet	• *What* questions • *look like* • Forms of verb	• Draw posters on pet-loving • Do pet survey	10 hours
	3	My School	• Basic adjectives • Present progressive	• Edit newspaper • Mime & guess	11 hours
Community	4	Mina is Visiting America	• How can I get _____? • Plural noun forms • There is/are	• Design a dream town • Study directions • Dictogloss	10 hours
	5	I love Cooking	• Cooking directions • Imperatives	• Do research on foods • run cooking class	10 hours
	6	Gestures	• Let's do ________. • Auxiliary *must*	• Different gestures • Gesture relay	9 hours
Enjoy Life	7	A Funny Story	• What a nice _____! • Thank you for ___. • Can I take _____?	• Collect cartoons • Draw a cartoon • Act out	10 hours
	8	What's Your Hobby?	• Hobby expressions • Gerund • Tag questions	• Talk about hobbies • Oral drill for tag	10 hours
	9	A Trip to Mountain Geumgang	• I'm going to ____. • It's sunny/cloudy.	• Make up itinerary • Forecast weather	10 hours

Now & Future	10	Let's Save the Earth	• by subway/bus • How often _____?	• Do survey on environment awareness	11 hours
	11	Our Hope & Dreams	• What questions • Why questions • To-infinitive	• Choose a job • Make field trip to offices	10 hours
	12	Internet Shopping	• Auxiliary *may* • and/but • Auxiliary *have to*	• Decide on key ten netiquettes & shopping tips	10 hours

Table 24 The Master Plan

1. Textbook	*Middle School English 1* (Published by Doosan)
2. Unit Title	Lesson 7: A Funny Story
3. General Objectives	
1) Main Objectives • Students can give simple descriptions of people and things. • Students can read and understand a funny story. • Students can make up a funny story in a cartoon format. 2) What to Learn (Language Functions) • to give thanks: *Thank you for coming.* • to make suggestions: *Can I take your coat?* • to use exclamative sentences: *What a nice party!* • to tell compliments: *The food is so delicious!* • to use past forms of verbs: *went, were, was, picked, poured.* 3) What to Do (Projects and Activities) • Students in groups collect cartoons (e.g.: Adam, Cathy, Garfield) on line. • Students in groups draw their own cartoon and act it out before the class.	
4. Reflection Questions	
• Are students interested enough to forget about the fact that they are learning English when making up a cartoon story? • How do the students respond to the American cartoons collected on line?	

Table 25 The Sub-plan

Lesson 7: A Funny Story		Page	Period
Warm Up, Let's Go, Listen and Talk ①		114-117	1/10
Aims	1. Students can describe people and things in the pictures. 2. Students can understand thanks, compliments, and suggestions. 3. Students can use interrogative and exclamative sentences correctly.		
Substep	Activities and Anticipated Problems		Input from Reflection
Introduction (3')	Guess the words that are used in a party situation		Brainstorm

Warm Up (6')		Look at the pictures on pp. 114-115 and find differences Divide class into 5 groups; encourage them to compete Retarded students might lose interest	Use no long sentences
Let's Go (15')	Look and Check (5')	When repeating, try accelerating the speed each time Add as many appropriate sentences as possible ex) The girl's hungry. (picture A) The man's drinking water. (picture B)	Examples must be real; Don't try to explain; Be brave
	Listen and Repeat (10')	Listen and repeat after tape in unison with loud voice Look at pictures and guess the meanings of dialogues Listen and repeat the sentences again, with emotion Encourage students to practice with fun; use humor	
Listen and Talk (18')	Listen and Answer (13')	Call on students; let them explain the situation in picture Let students listen to the tape and answer the questions Study the dialogue (Explain the concept of gerund) Listen to the dialogue again and do the role play	Prepare good examples with gerund in them
	Sounds (5')	Students will have difficulty learning the intonation with these: Can I **take** your **coat**? (↗) What are you **doing**? (↘) **What** a great **party**! (↘)	Make students intonation-sensitive
Consolidation (3')		Review the lesson with focus on descriptive words Let students fill in the blanks of Worksheet as homework Remind the class of the cartoon collection project	Don't try to review thoroughly

5.2 Tools for Activating the Reflection Phase

In every lesson, in every classroom, and in every school, events occur which the teacher can use to develop an understanding of his or her job. But teachers often fail to exploit these events, letting momentum of all the other events of the day take precedence. And yet these experiences can serve as the basis for the micro- and macro-reflection of the teacher if he or she knows ways to gather fuller information about the events. There are, by and large, six ways of doing this so that teachers can systematically develop strategies for their reflection, their planning, and their teaching. The six ways of promoting Reflective Language Teaching are:

(1) Writing teaching journals or logs. (These are written or recorded accounts of teaching experiences.)
(2) Preparing portfolios. (A portfolio is a purposeful collection of teacher work describing the efforts, progress, or achievement, together with the reflective journals.)
(3) Action research. ("research conducted in a field setting with those actually involved in that field, often alongside an 'outsider,' into the study of questions influenced by practitioners rather than solely by 'experts.'"[2])
(4) Talking with peers. (This can be done either informally or systematically; in the latter form it may lead to collaborative reflection.)
(5) Reading other teachers' stories of teaching. (It may involve reading outstanding teacher narratives or scanning peers' teaching logs.)
(6) Visiting other teachers' classrooms (It may imply either more formal imposed observation or informal visits.)

Of these, the first three are positive in that they require more commitment of teachers whereas the rest of the ways are less positive in that they may be carried out rather informally and less systematically. The first and the fifth approach seem to have a lot in common: they only differ in what is done to the

[2] Susan E. Noffke, 1997. In Hollingsworth (Ed.), *International action research: A casebook for educational reform*, 1997, p. 2.

Table 26 Desirable Method for Reflection

Items	Choices	Frequency	Percent
IV. 13. Desirable method or reflection	• writing teacher journal	10	11.4
	• sharing ideas with others	12	13.6
	• preparing a portfolio	33	37.5
	• success stories & episodes	9	10.2
	• microteaching	8	9.1
	• others	0	0
	• no response	16	18.2

content. In other words, one is writing the teacher stories while the other is reading them. So we may merge these two approaches into one: reading and writing teacher stories.

When asked "What would you rather do to be a reflective teacher?" the preservice and the inservice teachers in the survey of this study responded as follows:

To the question asked, the most answered was "preparing a portfolio," followed by "sharing ideas with others," followed by "writing teacher journal." If we combine the results of "writing teacher journal" and "success stories & episodes," the added frequency is 19, which ranks second, following the 33 of "preparing a portfolio." As a result, the two most desirable methods for reflection these preservice and inservice teachers think of are "preparing portfolios" and "reading and writing teacher stories."

Even though it could be the robustest method for teacher reflection, Korean teachers are hardly likely to prefer Action Research (AR). As Nunan (2001) points out, it is certainly not the case that "everything is rosy in the AR garden" (In Hall & Hewings (Eds.), 2001, p. 202). The principal problems identified by teachers who he has worked with include the following:

(1) Lack of time
(2) Lack of experience
(3) Fear of being revealed as an incompetent teacher
(4) Fear of producing a public account of their research for a wider (unknown) audience

Nunan (2001) maintains that he has experimented with a number of solutions to the problems, but none of them are convincing enough to recommend AR to Korean teachers as the essential method for their reflective teaching. Accordingly, the two robustest methods for reflection should be "preparing portfolios" and "reading and writing teaching journal," and these are the very approaches that we are going to adopt here for Korean EFL teachers' Reflective Language Teaching.

5.2.1 Writing Teaching Journal

With regard to reading outstanding teacher stories, Preskill & Jacobvitz (2001) highly recommend it to the teachers who want to find the teaching self and thereby grow professionally, with these words:

> The more we work with both novice and veteran teachers, the more we grow convinced that reading narratives written by skilled teacher-authors can greatly enhance understanding of teaching and learning. Expertly crafted stories of teaching portray classrooms in all their vivid and concrete particulars and offer both prospective and experienced teachers a vicarious means to face the challenges of educating children well. These narratives encourage teachers to educate more creatively and resourcefully, and they engender new hope about the impact

> of teachers' work. . . . Furthermore, these narratives are guides to living well. They show that to foster student growth, teachers must experience their own ongoing self-development—their own continuing educational renewal. Thus, great teaching grows out of a clear and often reinvented sense of self, and the most moving teacher narratives chronicle the emergence of a better self and a better teacher (p. 1).

This reminds us of Dewey (1916) when he said "The only adequate training for occupations is training through occupations" (p. 235). Reading other teachers' reflective stories is learning how to view, plan and do our teaching as well as how to reflect on it. And a possible result is that once they read the stories and get moved teachers want to write their own stories. So, for the teachers to develop the habit of writing a reflective journal or even a log or a note, there must be readable narratives around.

In this respect the educational society in Korea will likely have to create an atmosphere in which teachers write more freely. For, the reality is far from being a fertile soil for writing teaching journal either at school or on the Internet. One of the most well-known website for teachers in Korea, Edunet is running several bulletin boards for teachers who want to talk about their teaching life. There are some good teacher stories about class management or about ways to give pep talks to the students in charge. But, surprisingly, there are few articles found as far as teaching English is concerned. Nor are any good teaching stories of English language teachers in Korea found on-line. Only the voices of the commercially oriented teachers are reverberating throughout the Net, misleading students and other teachers to some dubious methodologies.

To correct this somewhat deformed situation and to maximize the potential of their teaching in the classroom, the English language teachers in Korea have to start writing reflective journal right away. When they write, the following reflection questions will perhaps be able to guide their journal entries:

Chart 4 Reflection Questions to Guide Journal Entries

Questions about what happened during a lesson

1. What was my idea for set induction? Was it appropriate?
2. What teaching materials did I use? Were they effective?
3. What language teaching techniques—cognitive, metacognitive, or affective—did I use?
4. Were my students able to achieve what they were supposed to achieve?
5. What kind of teacher-student interaction occurred?
6. Did anything amusing or unusual occur?
7. Which parts of the lesson were most successful?
8. Which parts of the lesson were least successful?
9. Would I teach the lesson differently if I taught it again?
10. What changes should I make in my teaching?

Questions about the students

1. Were students challenged by the lesson?
2. Did students contribute actively to the lesson?
3. What did they respond poorly to?

Questions to ask yourself as an English teacher

1. Do I enjoy teaching English?
2. Do the students enjoy my teaching English?
3. What are my strengths as an English teacher?
4. What are my limitations at present?
5. How can I improve my teaching English?
6. How can I help my students more?
7. Where am I in my professional development?

Teacher stories are typically written in a narrative genre. Preskill & Jacobvitz (2001) divide them into six types, which they claim represent important parts of the knowledge and dispositions preservice and inservice teachers should acquire to become better teachers (pp. 8-9). The six narrative types are:

1) narrative of social criticism; 2) narrative of apprenticeship and induction; 3) narrative of reflective practice; 4) narrative of journey; 5) narrative of hope; and 6) narrative of freedom. But this classification has little to do with the stories' real value and does not say much about how the stories are related to reflective teaching. For this reason the researcher should like to suggest another set of categories that will group the stories according to its reflective values. This set has five categories. They are:

(1) Macro factors. (Related to school, society, educational aims, curriculum and method)
(2) Micro factors (Related to classroom management, materials, motivation, and content)
(3) Planning factors (Related to general planning of ① lessons and units, ② organization, ③ lesson implementation, and ④ management)
(4) Teaching factors (Related to effectiveness, content-specific pedagogy, student learning in cognitive or affective areas, and assessment or evaluation)
(5) Reflection factors (Related to discovery of self, awareness of mannerism, successful and unsuccessful areas, value conflicts, and the extent of revision)

Based on these coding criteria, the following narrative of Bun-sug Kim (2001) can be classified as a micro teaching narrative with macro reflection overtones. Kim had kept a score of teaching journals between March 17, 1999 and July 14, 1999. She records in this diary her process of teaching English to her elementary school charges. A couple of sample journal entries read as follows:

The first class of lesson three. Saturday, April 10, 1999

Expressions like 'What are you wearing?' or 'I am wearing a blouse' seem to be rather difficult for kids, so it's probably the area that requires some practice.

As it was the first class, kids practiced new expressions and related words using pictures and realia before watching the video material. Supposedly, kids understand what's going on in the video show without any preliminary practice, but I saw them at a loss, not knowing how to answer when I asked them questions. So it seems to me that a bit of preliminary exercise helps them understand better. This time, however, all the pictures in the textbook were about phoning and there was no utilizing them so I was stuck. The only solution I came up with was to put Korean translation next to the dialogue of the first class. This idea was from the lecture of Suggestopedia I had once taken. I photocopied the dialogue to hand it out. For the kids who might feel anxiety about letters, I made it clear that the handouts were not for memorization, saying that they would have one more year to read those letters. I told them that just reading a few letters they already knew would be enough.

The fourth class of lesson four. May 12, 1999

When the kids engage in a language game, their faces reveal a lot of pleasure. There is no burdensomeness nor getting irritated in them.

Jinho has paid little attention all through this lesson and naturally he doesn't follow me even after practicing several times.

Today's game was about giving some information about our classmate to guess who. I let the students use the expressions we had practiced as much as possible, and had small group activities in order to engage all of them. (Author's translation)

This is a vivid description of English classrooms making the best of such detailed jargons as realia, preliminary exercise, Suggestopedia and anxiety. According to the above coding criteria, this reflective journal could be classified as mostly micro teaching and reflection though there are a few elements related to macro factors appearing on and off. Kim uses this diary, together with the children's diary about learning, to define the effect of teacher belief system on English instruction.

Francis Bacon quipped in his essay *Of Studies*, "Reading maketh a full man, conference a ready man, and writing an exact man. And therefore, if a man write little, he had need have a great memory; if he confer little, he had need have a present wit; and if he read little, he had need have more cunning, to seem to know that he doth not" (In Abrams et al. (Eds.), 1962, p. 1045). It is only natural that teachers make it a rule to keep a reflective journal to be a better practitioner. Teachers might complain that there is no time available with their hands full, but lest we should lose track of that valuable information we have gotten in the sea of oblivion we do well to start writing a reflective teaching journal. The praxis will surely pay off. If a teacher really has no time to write, however, then it will be sufficient to take a simple note in his or her notepad or keep a teaching log in any margin of the piece of paper at hand.

5.2.2 Preparing Portfolios

Another important tool in implementing Reflective Language Teaching is preparing a portfolio. While most of the teaching journals provide a vehicle for reflection on daily events or at least on the happenings over a not very long period of time, portfolios promote a broader perspective of the informants' teaching and philosophical beliefs collected over a long period of time (Borko et al, 1997; Yost et al., 2000).

Though there may be a number of variants in both of them, journal writing is fit for short-term micro-reflection whereas portfolio preparation is appropriate for long-term macro-reflection. Thus, these two robust forms of reflecting on teaching rightly constitute "the crouching tiger and the hidden dragon" to reflective practice, to borrow from Chinese metaphors. Underlying this methodological fortitude is perhaps the frequent recommendation of researchers on reflective teaching that the two means to effective reflection be developed and utilized among preservice or novice teachers in order to succeed in teacher training (Borko et al., 1997; Campbell et al., 2001; Carroll et al., 1996; Hamberger & Moore, 1997; McDermott et al., 1996; Yost et al., 2000).

Portfolio may sound vague to English teachers in Korea because the original meaning is often changed as each reader assimilates it into existing schemata. In Campbell et al. (2001), portfolios are subdivided into two categories: 1) a working portfolio and 2) a presentation portfolio. The former is always much larger and more complete than the latter, because it usually contains entire reflective journals, complete units, unique teacher-made materials, and a collection of videos. On the other hand, presentation portfolios are compiled for the purpose of giving others an effective and easy-to-read portrait of professional competence. They are usually more selective and streamlined, compared to the working portfolios. According to Carroll et al. (1996), however, portfolios come out in much more varying shapes and sizes, so they are best defined by their contents.

Creating a decent portfolio requires a great deal of time and hard work. The preparation of a good portfolio is especially important for the English teacher who is going to reflect on what he or she did over a certain period of time to teach students the portions of English as specified in the syllabus or the lesson plan. The typical entries in the portfolio of English teachers in Korea will perhaps include the following items:

(1) Teaching journals or logs
(2) Teaching materials developed (flash cards, experience charts, magazine pictures)
(3) Feedback from learners (student diaries, surveys and questionnaires, letters, bulletin board ideas, student portfolios)
(4) Syllabuses, lesson plans, or lesson reports
(5) Multimedia sources (CD-ROMs, audio or video tapes, slides, Internet files)
(6) Other planning or teaching related materials (anecdotal articles or records, essays, theme studies, field trip plans)
(7) Evaluations (observation reports, peer critiques, awards, personnel statements)

Carefully prepared portfolios will help document teachers' learning, growth, and professional development over time. Teachers are also able to gain a vision of the world of teaching as they build a record of their professional growth in a portfolio. Besides, as they engage in portfolio development, teachers are able to gain a clear picture of themselves finding out their strengths and weaknesses as an emerging professional. Due to these benefits, portfolios have recently received increasing attention as tools to promote reflection among both experienced and novice teachers (Borko et al., 1997; Richert, 1990). Many empirical studies of portfolios consistently argue that the tool appears to foster teacher reflection in that it helps teachers to remember classroom events more fully and accurately, and focused their reflections on content and content-specific aspects of their teaching.

5.3 Individual vs. Collective Reflection

According to Apanakhi Buckley (2000) from Heritage College, there are two types of society with respect to collective behavior; one society is described as having the "argument culture" in which criticism, attack, or opposition are the predominant ways of responding to people or ideas (p. 145). In such a society, participants become increasingly aware of their differences and the areas in which their understandings are shared, as the discussion progresses. They perform the so-called argument building. In this dialogic act of discourse, the more possible it is for participants to make assumptions explicit, the more successful the argument will be. People build on each other's ideas, constructing a palpable new reality between them. The effect of the discussion is thus positive. But the resultant confrontation does not always yield a positive outcome. It could be negative. But whether the outcomes of discussion are positive or negative, this model of discussion characterizes the Western society in general, and the United States in particular.

On the opposite side lies the other society in which there is not much confrontation and hence no argument nor much discussion. One person may speak for five minutes or he may speak for an hour. All the other members listen because what is being said is for the benefit of the group. This characterizes the "talking circle" of Blackfoot people, a tribe of native Americans (Ibid., p. 146). Talking circle is a native American way of considering important issues and getting the input of everyone. People sit in a circle so that every body can be seen. Each person in the circle takes a turn talking. Usually, when each person has spoken, they come to a group conclusion. Maybe somebody presents a summary and everybody consents. It sounds much like a "talking circle" called *bansanghoi* that takes place to discuss local matters about once a month in an urban block as well as in a rural village in Korea.

Current definitions of reflection are strongly influenced by the Western cultural heritage in that they heavily draw on the whole span of western philosophical thoughts ranging from Socrates to Kant to Dewey. Individual reflection seems to operate much the same way across cultures; however, collaborative reflection differs from culture to culture from Buckley's (2000) point of view. Let's discuss more fully here these two different types of reflection.

Individual reflection involves a lot of thinking, so it is even compared to Zen Buddhist mindfulness by Tremmel (1993). He contends that Schönian reflection, especially his concept of reflection-in-action, and the *zazen* of Zen philosophy share an important common ground. According to Tremmel, Zenists' mindfulness means to "pay attention to right here, right now" and to invest the present moment with "full awareness and concentration" (Ibid., p. 443). As Hackett (1979) gives words to its origin, the basic ideas of Zen were brought to China in the sixth century.

Like all Buddhism, this version emphasized the decisive importance of rigorous self-discipline and fully-controlled contemplation as means of achieving enlightenment. So, to find the truth a man need consult no book or treatise of philosophy; it is only necessary instead to look with the "right eyes" into his own heart to discover the "undifferentiable oneness of all reality with the Buddha-nature" (p. 102). In Zenists' thought true knowledge is to be found in the very place where all the distinctions of analytic reason have disappeared. This might be the ultimate stage that the power of individual reflection can reach.

Collective reflection begins with individuals who are willing to leave their comfort zone in order to change and mature. It thrives on the argument culture. For the result of reflection to be of any effectiveness, there must be some confronting because it is a step in revealing the nature of forces that inhibit and constrain teachers (Smyth, 1989). The constructive act of confronting is nothing less than investigating the larger social, cultural, and political contexts in which policies and theories are developed. It is an indispensible quality for macro-reflection. Therefore, confrontation, argument, and people building on each other's ideas should characterize the fruitful collective macro-reflection. However, respecting the silence of the reserved members is also the spirit of successful collective reflection.

And just with this spirit Korean school administrators should rouse themselves to support and sustain teacher development over time by experimenting with such new conceptions and practices as situated cognition, critical dyads, teacher development and/or teacher research groups, and educational reform networks, to maximize the potentials of this new collective leadership. Otherwise, school systems that are usually organized bureaucratically and function traditionally will have difficulty adapting to change or accommodating to these new conditions. Let's look into these new conceptions of collective reflection in more detail.

First of all, situated cognition is "a means to make explicit the typically tacit knowledge of expert teachers and place beginning teachers' knowledge-in-action at the center of the learning-to-teach process" (Ethell & McMeniman, 2000, p. 90). In this view knowledge is created and made meaningful by the context and activities through which it is acquired. And the cognitive apprenticeship learning model based on this concept enables powerful links to be forged between learning and doing. It is a kind of cognitive intervention that is conceptualized within a framework of situated cognition and reflective practice. Ethell & McMeniman report on a teaching approach derived from this cognitive apprenticeship where novice teachers get access to the thinking underlying the practice of one expert teacher.

The concept of critical dyad comes from a paper which reports on a critical friendship between a female teacher of English for Academic Purposes (EAP) and a researcher who teaches in the English Teacher Education Program of the National Institute of Education, Singapore. The critical friendship begins when the former asks the latter to observe her classes. For the facilitation of collaborative reflection data are collected by: 1) classroom observation notes; 2) individual meetings; 3) audio recordings of meetings, and video recordings of classes; 4) the teacher's written reactions to her classes and e-mail correspondence. The most significant finding is that the person who is reflecting should be in a good personal psychological state in order to be able to confront any inconsistencies that may occur.

Finally, educational reform networks or collaboratives are teacher-led organizations that, are "loose, borderless, and flexible, and are particularly well suited to this era of new technology and rapid change" (Lieberman, 2000, p. 221). These networks are organized around the interests and needs of their participants, building agendas sensitive to their individual and collective development as teachers. With a remarkable maneuverability and creativity, they can change quickly and invent new structures and activities that are responsive to their members.

For decades in the United States, scores of school-improvement networks have been activated. Five key characteristics of the 60 networks studied are identified as: 1) a strong sense of commitment to an idea; 2) a sense of shared purpose; 3) a mixture of information sharing and psychological support; 4) a facilitator who ensured voluntary participation and equal treatment; and 5) an egalitarian ethos (Lieberman, Ibid., p. 222).

In a nutshell, the networks are run with the spirit of volunteerism and democracy which most of the Korean in-service teacher training programs seem to be lacking. And there is one significant phenomenon that the American networks show which requires Korean teacher educators' attention. Some of these U.S. organizations seek to promote many important goals including literacy and student-centered education, using charismatic leaders or promoting dialogue between university and school personnel. However, it is reported that most of the networks that hold their members and continue to attract new teachers try their best to account for the daily pressures of teaching, even as they seek to advance larger ideals.

In a democratic society, this type of collaborative reflection can do many things. It may well have a healing effect on the possible dogmatic attitude that a reflective individual might end up with. It may well give a good number of participants an opportunity to share with the valuable understanding or awareness that the individual reflection must bring about. Although both types of reflection could be described as having the commitment to truth or as an effort to find the best solution to immediate problems facing a teacher, individual reflection is much like a journey into self while collaborative reflection tends to demand the individuals to come forward with the spirit of confrontation, which means a lot of courage or a great deal of commitment to truth in their own culture.

To successfully implement the ideal of the collaborative reflection which apparently has a host of merits, ELT educators in Korea do well to take into consideration the feasibility and viability of such new conceptions as situated cognition, critical dyads, teacher development groups, collaboratives or educational reform networks the key characteristics of which are delineated above. One last question to ask here in relation to individual and collaborative reflection is, What are the good school systems that foster such virtues of reflection?

As pointed out in Newman and Wehlage (1995), a self-conscious professional community is a salient characteristic of those schools most successful with students. A self-conscious professional community means that in such community teachers pursue a clear and shared purpose for all student learning, engage in collaborative activity to achieve that purpose, and take collective responsibility for their students' learning. This could be one sure way of preventing the decay of any schools.

5.4 A New Empowered Vision of Teaching English

Since the English language was first taught in Dongmunhak in 1883 by foreigners using the rudimentary doctrines of the Direct Method, there have been a number of language teaching approaches implemented or tried out in Korea. The most prominent among them are Grammar-Translation Method (GTM), Audio-Lingual Method (ALM), and Communicative Language

Teaching (CLT). These three teaching methods were introduced one by one in the 120-year-old history of English language teaching in Korea, but as of now they should be thought of as coexisting in the minds of the English language teachers on site.

The survey results we have already examined in Chapter Three tell us that both the preservice and the inservice teachers do not even slightly hesitate to support the purely behavioristic conception of teaching while supporting the humanistic and constructivist ideas of teaching theoretically opposed to behavioristic thinking. Another interesting finding was that participants responded quite positively to the question whether or not acquiring an automatic linguistic habit through repetition drills is important in EFL learning.

According to the survey, quite a number of respondents believe that Behaviorism or Audiolingualism is no bad theory in teaching and/or learning English. This attitude is perhaps due to their own teaching and learning experiences; otherwise, they would not have answered positively against their knowledge that either the Behavioristic practices or the Audio-Lingual ways of learning English are out of fashion and are currently being discouraged from implementing it.

CLT can be said to be the dominant methodology in Korea now. The survey results show that inservice teachers' use of games and experience in TPR is rather high with the mean score 3.61 and 3.03 respectively. These types of classroom activity will lead the language teachers to zero in on certain communicative goals. Most teaching recommendations are faithfully following the doctrine of CLT. Apparently, CLT has a lot of strengths. The desired outcome is that the learner can communicate successfully in the target language in real situations, rather than have a conscious understanding of the rules governing that language.

This methodological focus on communication, however, could constitute not only its strength but also its weakness. In an ESL situation there are ample opportunities for learners to practice the language by using it for real communication; however, in an EFL situation there are only sparse chances for learners to use the language for real communication, say, with English-speaking foreigners. In reality they can have a travesty of communication through the so-called "communicative" exercises in the book or through the "communicative" activities used in the classroom or in their homework assignment.

The amount of language input the EFL learners are supposed to get cannot possibly be compared with that of their ESL brothers and sisters educated in English-spoken countries. The former are exposed only to four to five hours a week at school although many of them also go to a private language institute to "study" English. Given this rather poor learning environment, it is small wonder that they view the Audio-lingual method of overlearning and hard practice as the most attractive and practical solution to their immediate need to master even the "rules" of language which will guide them to construe the meaning of the target language sentences.

In this regard, it appears that the shadow of GTM also looms long and strong. In the elementary classroom, English seems to be taught and learned along the line of activity-based CLT methodology, which continues smoothly into the curriculum of middle school juniors. However, teaching the middle school seniors and the levels of students upward, namely, the high school students and even the college students is a different tale to be reeled off. The learners at these levels feel extremely stressed under the burden of upcoming examinations.

To get ahead in the examinations there should be no waste

of time nor any waste of effort. The economic principle predominates in this learning market. Consequently, the teachers and the students have no other alternative but to choose the Grammar-Translation Method, the most "effective" but the most mistreated methodology. Many theorists warn that GTM approaches to language learning deductively rather than inductively and that it separates the grammatical forms from communicative meaning. Tens of thousands of Korean (or Asian) teachers and learners cannot be entirely wrong, however.

To succeed in the examination or to go through the society-created ritual of passage whether it is for college entrance or for getting a job, the teachers and the learners have chosen the best possible method that they believe to be the most effective and rewarding means for their goal. If their choice is theoretically wrong, the first to be blamed will be the system of examination. But, can we rightly say that the examination system is entirely wrong? Any reasonable person has to face the reality. The system of examination is the reality and perhaps the best solution we have come up with so far.

Based on the perceptions of the survey participants of this study and on the analysis above, an important rationale of Reflective Language Teaching should be geared to the needs of eclecticism in English language instruction in Korea. One method or approach alone cannot fully cover the vast realm that the multifaceted problems of Korean ELT linger around and occupy. Taking this into account, we can be about to understand why the preservice and inservice teachers showed a slice of their behavioral paradox that they quite willingly accept both of the methodological nemeses, namely, ALM and CLT, behaviorism and humanism, authority and democracy, and finally, conservatism and liberalism.

Reflective Language Teaching is more a pedagogical methodology than a language teaching methodology. Its main tenet is that, like the ant in the parable, the reflective language teacher should diligently bring the "ears of corn" (the merits and strengths of all other language teaching methodologies) to the "nest" (the classroom or the skills inventory of the teacher). Therefore, the view of a diligent, hard-working teacher and the thought of enthusiasm and commitment as its prime virtue are somewhat acerbic but to the point. For, RLT is not a one-time-basis practice nor the "one size fits all" methodology. Its development process is a spiral development while its three-step or seven-phase process of one cycle is to be cyclically unfolded, as we have already seen in Chapter Four.

RLT is to operate over a long period of teaching life. As those five, ten, fifteen or twenty years of spiral development take place and add up the effects, the language teacher will be growing and changing before reaching the stance of the *myeong-in* (in Korean) or *meijin* (in Japanese) at last. This is a truly empowering vision of a language teacher, for it is no impractical or impossible vision of an ordinary teacher with a modest desire and ambition. It not only makes the teacher really help the learner or learners but also enriches the teacher's own professional life. For such a teacher there is only one reward to seek after: being truly useful to his or her students and being appreciated. The best remuneration for any teacher will be the simple two words "thank you." They are simple but powerful because they amount to a symbolic gesture indicating the existence of successful give-and-take.

Let's summarize the characteristics of RLT that have been discussed so far: first, RLT pursues eclecticism; second, RLT is a long-term methodology; third, RLT prizes feedback. The other characteristics of RLT can be feature-marked as follows:

Chart 5 The Distinctive Features of Reflective Language Teaching

Areas	**Features of Reflective Language Teaching**		
Educational Philosophy:	[-dogmatic]	[+eclectic]	[-top-down]
View of Language:	[+meaning-based]	[+behavioristic]	[+form-focused]
Process of Teaching:	[-routine]	[+plan-oriented]	[+experiential]
View of Learning:	[+teacher-centered]	[+learner-centered]	[+ZPD-oriented]
Scopes of Reflection:	[+school-based]	[+collaborative]	[+society-oriented]

A lot of more features may well be marked with the criteria added. The main thing, however, is that RLT is a method of language teaching taking into consideration as many variables as possible in order to come up with a maximally appropriate methodology of teaching in a given situation. So, Reflective Language Teaching can be called Appropriate Language Teaching or Proper Language Teaching. According to the *Webster's New International Dictionary*, the English word 'appropriate' comes from the Latin verb *appropriare* which means 'to make peculiarly the possession of someone.' RLT is a method of English language teaching by means of which the teacher makes English peculiarly the possession of the learners. In this process of "peculiar" adaption to teaching English, the gap between the top-down theories and the practices of classroom teaching can be bridged in any significant form.

Reflective Language Teaching is for change and for awakening. And it is a means to catalyzing the reform of English language teaching in Korea. The seven hallmarks of a robust RLT can be summarized as follows:

(1) RLT enhances the personal awareness of the act of teaching.
(2) RLT materializes the vague concepts and abstruse theories with the situation-specific ideas and data, thereby preventing the theory/practice divide that may well take place

at the end of the consumer line.

(3) RLT promotes the continuous development of on-site teachers to the extent that they find their teaching life full of worth and reward.

(4) RLT enables the teachers to experience the collaborative and/or interactive learning by implementing the reflective practice not only alone but also in dyads and groups so as to receive the transfusion of a variety of ideas and facilitate their professional development.

(5) RLT will have effect on the formation of educational policy and on the practice of top-down intervention by encouraging the teachers in bottom-up theorizing and decision-making so that a desirable "grass-roots" reform may be launched.

(6) The students will find and appreciate the pleasure of learning, discovery, development, and growth through the bettered classroom teaching balanced and harmonized and believe in the value of public schooling instead of private schooling so that the decay of the school can be prevented as the public schooling is in full operation.

(7) The teachers will find themselves at the rank of major professionals due to the experiential and procedural knowledge base they obtain on site and with the hard-won dignity they will contribute to society and be able to lead a life of true value. In sum, they will enjoy a happy teaching life, being a self-confident, creative, respected craft-professional free from complacency and routinized practice.

5.5 The Usability of the RLT Model

The best possible model for implementing RLT in Korean

contexts has already been introduced in Chapter Four. The two basic schemata were used to delineate the three-phase reflective teaching model and its enlarged form incorporating the macro-factors. The present chapter has introduced another model where the Teaching Phase receives input from both the Planning Phase and the Reflection Phase. Now, an important question arises. Will the proposed RLT models be implemented in Korean ELT situations with maximum usability? To address this problem of feasibility, the researcher will return to the survey analysis briefly. For, the re-examination of the survey results will show the crucial teacher beliefs that will provide the sturdy bases for the RLT model implementation in Korean grade school situations.

First of all, one of the most important findings was that the teachers do not think teaching is an easy job. To the question "How advanced a teacher are you?" the majority of the subjects answered that they think they are average. Even the majority of the inservice teachers do not seem to believe that they are up to the level of experts. To the question "What is the requirement of being an expert?" 35.2% of them picked "hard work for good teaching" for their answer. What could specifically be meant by "hard work" in this context? It might refer to a thorough preparation for good teaching and a conscientious self-reflection after teaching. Understandably, only 2.3% of the respondents chose "linguistics and pedagogy" as the requirement of being an expert. The teachers seemed to be well aware that acquiring the knowledge alone would not do a good job in teaching English.

All of these perceptions of the not-yet-achieved professional masterfulness will surely lead the Korean English language teachers to support a teacher development program which both focuses on planning and facilitates a steady self-reflection on teaching practices. This supportive attitude of the teachers is also expected from the survey result that the respondence is very positive to the questions asking of the teachers' need to change and grow more. And this is probably why the majority of the subjects showed their strong belief in the usefulness of critical reflection to the question asking if it will be greatly helpful to understand their teaching techniques.

Secondly, another important finding was that the teachers want to receive a substantial psychological reward. They secretly wish to be treated as a person with authority. Therefore, they responded quite positively to the question asking of the usefulness of the traditional idea of king-teacher-father trinity. It is very unlikely that the teachers have a reactionary tendency, though. They are only trying to find their professional identity in the relationship between the students and themselves, thereby regaining the teacher's authority. They well know, however, that a true respect from the students cannot be afforded by the by-gone ideology and that the method and content of their teaching as well as its quality will ultimately matter. Even though they are unable to name it exactly, they already sense that what the RLT models imply is what they need to pursue to upgrade their teaching.

Thirdly, the majority of the respondents answered that the most important quality of an English teacher should be "enthusiasm and commitment." Also, to the question "What is the ideal image of an English teacher?" they answered that "the culture-developing teacher focusing on holistic development" would be one. They seem to believe that an English teacher as a knowledge-giver is an old-timer's idea. That an English teacher should aim to develop the holistic personality of his or her students rather than simply teaching the skills of English could be a therapeutic thought for Korea's thwarted ELT agenda.

RLT looks out upon a better condition for English education. Its legitimate means is through a constant self-reflection. So long as the goal of the Korean English teachers is to help students get deeper understanding rather than simple analytical knowledge of English, one might say that the tenets of RLT fit perfectly here.

Another basis for successful RLT implementation in Korea is that the Korean English teachers seem to be looking for a good eclectic bottom-up methodology. The survey results of the third section on classroom behavior mostly showed that the teachers are looking for ways to diversify their methodological outlook. They seem quite ready to accept varied teaching methods and techniques as long as they prove effective in their teaching and learning English. But the survey results also showed that some methods including TPR do not enjoy a high degree of recognition among Korean English teachers even though they are quite popular abroad and, especially TPR, regarded as a good way of implementing the Communicative Approach (Krashen and Terrell, 1983, p. 77). The use of the Internet and of the computer courseware is another area that needs further exploration. In sum, the practice of RLT will surely help the teachers broaden their methodological horizon and adapt to any "new" ways of teaching English.

Finally, the survey results of the fourth section on reflective self-development showed that the majority of the subjects are already practicing reflection on their teaching. This is very stimulating in that there will hardly be any significant resistance to the full implementation of the RLT methodology. But it was also revealed that the ways of reflection adopted are yet negative—the rate of experience in reflective journal is still very low with the mean score of 2.61 and the rate of experience in reading a vivid description of teaching life is also rather low with the mean score of 2.86. And the majority of the subjects responded to the question asking of their teaching style by picking up "diligent worker" for their answer choice while only 26.1% answered they believed that they are "creative problem-solvers."

All of these findings indicate that the Korean English teachers are well readied to accept the RLT methodology and that there are a lot of rooms for them to improve themselves in view of true implementation of the RLT models proposed in this study. Thus, one may safely say that the proposed RLT models are highly feasible given the revealed educational mood of ELT in Korea.

5.6 Implications for Teacher Education

The teachers in the first line often voice their complaint that the curriculum for teacher education (TE) is not very systematic and too much focused on theories that are separated from reality (Jung, 2001; Kang, 2001). The result of the survey of this study also showed that the inservice teachers are not much satisfied with the TE programs. To the question "What is the most urgent need to improve the inservice teacher training programs?" the majority of the inservice teachers (20 out of 38 teachers) answered "lack of systematic training." Such perceptions of inservice teachers are most probably due to the fact that the inservice teacher training is fitted in not to the real needs of the teacher-learners but to much of the demonstration effect of new educational policy or to the administrative expediency. The best solution, therefore, is to eliminate or at least minimize the [+top-down] elements from the whole curriculum so as to chisel out a sufficiently learner-centered curriculum.

It is also of much urgency that the teachers themselves not favor enhancing such personal proficiency training as increasing conversational or communicative abilities or other English-related courses but have opportunities to deeply reflect upon what really happens in their classrooms or what it really means to teach English to Korean students "now and here." Then, the teacher-learners do well to have a variety of collaborative reflective meetings either in pairs or in groups to fully discuss the implications of their reflection on teaching. However, the illusion that we will be able to change the whole situation once and for all should be thwarted. In their journal writing or preparing for portfolios, or in their individual or collaborative reflections the teachers and the teacher educators may consider the following rationales of Reflective Language Teaching this study has proposed so far:

1. Proposed as a language teaching methodology, RLT feeds an inquiring mind that makes the person concerned adhere to the problem until it is finally coped with. It draws on the ancient methodology of looking for solutions by utilizing the unique intellectual capacity of man. Teacher educators should therefore allow the teacher learners to enjoy the maximum freedom of choice with regard to picking up their methodology in teaching.
2. Teachers' core values, their belief system, attitudes and philosophy all influence and contribute to classroom teaching. In brief, the educational philosophy of English language teachers in Korea is something akin to eclecticism. They are pragmatists. They believe in the benefits of Communicative Approach and at the same time they believe in the apparent strength of Behavioristic doctrines.

It will be of no use, therefore, to make them partial to any special methodology for their classroom action.

3. Authenticity should be reinterpreted in that the "authentic" materials imported directly from English-spoken countries should be our food for thought. Korean English teachers or teacher educators had best inquire into the "learnability" and "teachability" of the so-called "authentic" materials. And we have to view the problem of authenticity in the World English (WE) perspective (Kimberley Brown, 2001. In Hall & Hewings, 2001, pp. 108-117). If there is such thing as Singaporean or Malaysian English, there could be Japanese or Korean English as well.
4. The nature of language and its acquisition is far more complex than anyone possibly thinks. In order to teach students how to share and negotiate the meaning or conventions of English, therefore, English language teachers need to implant an "empathy" skill. The holistic approach takes a firm stand in this respect. One good reminder is that to teach a foreign language in this manner will surely require of the language teacher the highest teaching skills or expertise ever thought of.
5. RLT and CLT or other contemporary language teaching methodologies with similar rationales are not mutually exclusive. Rather, they share whatever strengths and merits they have. They are complementary in the sense that RLT ultimately needs to adapt itself to a Korean version of CLT. For, CLT is a robust theory of language teaching and learning in which a number of breakthroughs from modern applied linguistics and liberal sciences such as sociolinguistics and constructive psychology are found as its constructs.

6. Why should the teachers use RLT? A common teacher's understanding of classroom experience is rather synthetical than analytical and not rich or detailed enough to drive systematic reflection. So an intentional reflection is needed to empower the teacher to plan effectively and teach with easiness. Through active reflection teachers become empowered teachers who then turn into transformative intellectuals who are endowed with skills of critical reflectivity and enlightened attitudes toward societal and educational reforms.
7. Individual reflection involves a lot of thinking, so it is even compared to Zen Buddhist mindfulness. Like all Buddhism, this version emphasized the decisive importance of rigorous self-discipline and fully-controlled contemplation as means of achieving enlightenment. So, to find the truth a man need consult no book or treatise of philosophy; it is only necessary instead to look with the "right eyes" into his own heart to discover the truth. As elucidated above, this is the ultimate stage that the power of individual reflection can reach.
8. Collective or collaborative reflection thrives on the argument culture. Schools and TE administrators should support this culture at every educational level. They should also sustain teacher development over time by experimenting with situated cognition, critical dyads, teacher development groups, and educational reform networks, to maximize the potentials of a new collective leadership that can be reaped from it.

Finally, any approaches to good English language teaching in Korea must be concerned with the fact that the teachers are already full-loaded with their tasks. They are prone to avoid any extra burden. Introducing RLT should not be such that it will be the straw that finally broke the camel's back. It should be such that the users will find a practical value in it and that they will find it worthwhile to adopt this approach to their teaching. The teachers need to be persuaded that it could save their time and make them successful.

VI. CONCLUSION

The general direction of educational policies and research agendas of Korean ELT has been much too dependent on one methodology, that is, Communicative Language Teaching. There is no doubt that CLT is a robust method with a magnificent theoretical basis, but historically it was born in the process of addressing the ESL teaching problems. A language-oriented methodology in its embryonic development, CLT has so many realistic constraints that it can hardly be the methodological mainstay by itself at grade school English classrooms in Korea. In our neighboring countries in-depth researchers witness that the purport of new CLT curricula is not carried out very well in the classroom level. Considering that the ELT environment of these countries is not drastically different from that of ours, caution must be used as to accepting a rash or unstrung optimism concerning the implementation of CLT in Korea.

Another significant problem this study has pointed out is that the conceptual understandings of the principles of CLT such as authenticity and meaningfulness are interpreted in an all-or-nothing pattern, and that the lopsided emphasis on the urgent mastery of the target language tends to drive the teachers into a narrow stance. Losing more and more of their ground and taking less and less of their initiative, the English language teachers in Korea are in confusion concerning how to teach. Already beset by dozens of mind-numbing problems at school and in the classroom, they are not at all sure that CLT or other communication-based teaching methodologies are really effective and attractive enough to replace the ALM or GTM practices which are deemed antique but which they feel more secure with.

This study has addressed these perceived problems by making the best use of the pedagogy-based teaching methodology called "reflective teaching." Furthermore, teaching has a number of variables: goals, curriculum, method, teacher, learner, school, and society. Among the variables what has received the main focus of this study was teacher. What does he or she do to teach the students the English language that seems hard to learn? What is his or her role to implement the proposed RLT model in order to successfully indigenize the CLT methodology in Korean grade school English classrooms? To address these questions, the study has referred to the pedagogical conception of "reflective practitioner" which has been quite popular among the teachers and teacher educators in the English-spoken countries but rarely discussed in Korean contexts.

The study has thus considered the ways to develop a Reflective Language Teaching model which will hopefully provide a working model for English language teachers in Korea as to how to teach English in Korean contexts in a most effective and successful manner. For this purpose, the study has examined a series of questions which underpin a teacher competency agenda, such as what exactly is reflective thinking, how teachers are supposed to perform this rather "new" skill, what beliefs and attitudes they have for the present, and what implications the answers to these questions have for teacher education? The study has approached these questions in terms of an educational model development, referring to the evidence from related literature and drawing on the results of a questionnaire survey. The main focus of the study was on establishing the theoretical foundations, on securing the identification of local contexts, and on discovering the ideal structural form of the reflective language teaching model, drawing on the theory of reflection.

After reviewing the literature, a descriptive survey was administered and analyzed to provide the basis for the reflective teaching model to be developed. To sum up, both preservice and inservice teachers believe that the job of teaching is not so prestigious as that of a doctor or of a lawyer but that it is becoming a rather popular job nowadays. They also seemed to feel that their self-esteem needs to be boosted in one way or another and that accepting the seemingly opposed ways of teaching such as Behaviorism and Constructivism or ALM and CLT are not contradictory at all, which proves nothing but their preference to methodological eclecticism or pragmatism. The subjects seemed to well recognize the importance of school culture in relation to teacher development and they answered that preparing for portfolios would be the best possible way of promoting reflectivity among the Korean English teachers, although they confessed that they were using a rather negative way of implementing RLT in reality, that is, sharing ideas with others.

In Chapter IV, the rationales and assumptions of Reflective Language Teaching were introduced before the structural nature of RLT was defined along with the procedural descriptions of the RLT models. The crucial tenet or doctrine for RLT can be summarized as inquisitive, eclectic, and pragmatic. It goes for multiple perspectives to the problems of language teaching and learning. It denies any affiliation to a particular method. It aims to find the best solution for a particular teacher to teach a particular lesson to a particular group of learners in a language classroom. Thus the proposed RLT model is teacher-oriented, because it involves teachers planning their lesson, making decisions, and taking actions before collecting data about their own classrooms and their roles within them, and using that data as a basis for self-evaluation and for professional growth.

The first cyclic model consists of three phases: planning, teaching, and reflection. This model can be extended to involve not only the micro factors such as classroom teaching but also the macro factors including school and society variables. The final model addressing both micro and macro factors requires seven phases to constitute one full cycle. In this model, the operation of the model has been defined as cyclic because each module has to be fed into one another. With the focus on Teaching, however, it could be said that Teaching receives input from both sides, from Planning and Reflection. So, to activate the Teaching Phase both the Planning Phase and the Reflection Phase have been urged to be activated first. In view of this, a sample RLT syllabus has been designed to exemplify the activation of the Planning Phase and the two most desirable methods for reflection, "preparing portfolios" and "reading and writing teacher stories" have been adopted to promote reflectivity among English language teachers in Korea.

One of the many rationales provided in this study is an answer to the question: Why should we adopt Reflective Language Teaching? The presented answer is: "It is because reflection is the path to deeper understanding of the instructional practice." A common teacher's understanding of classroom experience is rather synthetical than analytical and not rich or detailed enough to drive systematic reflection. So an intentional reflection is needed to empower the teacher to plan effectively and teach with easiness. There seems to be no legitimate excuse that teachers can make in order to avoid this sort of reflection now. The problem, therefore, is not whether we have to reflect on our teaching practice or not but what we have to reflect on it how. As we go on, however, we encounter a much more difficult problem which is not as much related to the quantity of reflection as to the quality of reflection. At some juncture, how much we reflect will be far less significant than what exactly we reflect on and how well we reflect on it.

In the end the degree of appropriateness and the degree of being to the point will determine everything. This is just why Reflective Language Teaching could be called "Appropriate Language Teaching." Reflective Language Teaching is a method of English language teaching by means of which the teacher makes English peculiarly the possession of the learner or learners. In this process of "peculiar" adaption or accommodation of teaching English, the gap between the imported, top-down theories of methodologies and the practice of actual classroom teaching can be bridged in any significant degree or form. Therefore, Reflective Language Teaching is for change, for awakening, and for catalyzing the reform of English language teaching in Korea. The seven hallmarks of a robust RLT which have been summarized in the last chapter are thus of much significance.

Seen from a slightly different angle, the goal of RLT is to enhance the personal awareness of the act of teaching. It materializes the vague concepts and abstruse theories with the situation-specific ideas and data, thereby preventing the theory/practice divide that may well take place at the receiving end of the transaction. It also promotes the continuous development of on-site teachers to the extent that they find their teaching life full of worth and reward. By receiving the transfusion of a variety of ideas which will facilitate the teachers' professional development, RLT will also have effect on the formation of educational policy and on the forms of top-down intervention. The teachers will now take initiative in bottom-up theorizing and decision-making so that a desirable "grass-roots" reform may be launched. And in the fruits of the reform the students will find the pleasure of learning through the bettered classroom life and they will believe in public schooling more than in private schooling. The decay of the school should be prevented as long as the former is in full operation.

To conclude: All the language-based methodologies will come and go with no exception of CLT, but the basic propositions of RLT will die hard since its rationales are deeply rooted in the time-honored practice of discovering truth that dates back to as early as the days of Socrates. RLT is a method tested in the process of a long period of time. Without regard to this universal and fundamental problem-solving capacity of mankind, there is no way of coping with the devilishly intertwined problems of English language education in Korea. To best implement the truly learner-centered English curriculum, to best fit the strengths of newly introduced post-CLT methodologies including TBL and TBT, and to wisely indigenize all the imported language teaching methodologies, the ancient but revisited method of Reflective Language Teaching should be utilized to the utmost. For, with this new empowered vision, we Korean teachers will soon start seeking solutions not from top to bottom but from bottom to top either in individuals or in dyads or in groups for the successful language teaching in the 21st-century English classrooms.

Appendix

A Survey on the Perceptions and Opinion of Their Job and View of Reflective Self-development of Korean English Teachers

The purpose of this survey is to find out how the English teachers in Korea understand their job, what educational philosophy and view of ideal teacher they hold, and how they endeavor to achieve self-development so as to succeed in their profession. After carefully reading the following questionnaire, choose and mark the appropriate number on the blank provided, according to the level of your agreement for each item. The bigger the number, the stronger the agreement.

1	2	3	4	5
absolutely not true	not true	so-so	true	absolutely true

Also, for the multiple-choice items, you may either choose and mark the number of your choice among the examples or, if there is no favorite of yours, write in the parentheses what you think appropriate.

I. View of Teaching

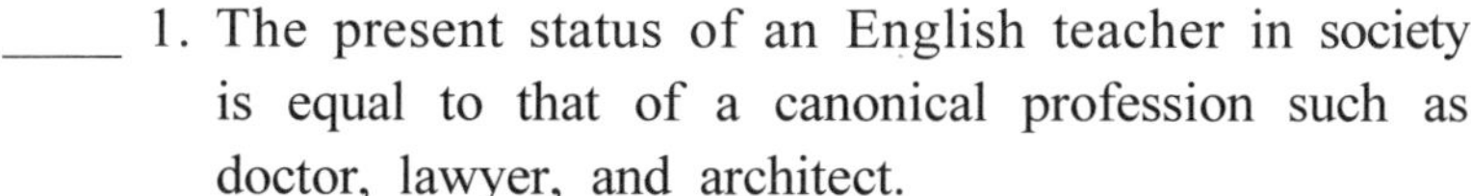

____ 1. The present status of an English teacher in society is equal to that of a canonical profession such as doctor, lawyer, and architect.

____ 2. Nowadays teaching is one of the most popular and

appealing profession.

____ 3. I am respected by the students I teach.

____ 4. I became or will become the English teacher that I have wanted to be.

____ 5. Teachers have no autonomy at all; every decision is made by outside conditions and social policies.

____ 6. In the level of an English teacher, there seems to be a series of developmental stages including novice, average, advanced, and superlative.

____ 7. What do you think is the greatest impediment in the professional development of an English teacher?
① alienation from society ② stress from identity crisis) ③ conflict with administrators ④ budget deficiency and lack of support ⑤ bad educational conditions and lack of high-tech facilities ⑥ lack of consolidation and communication between teachers ⑦ others (   )

____ 8. If you think there is a series of developmental stages, what stage do you suppose you are in?
① novice ② average ③ advanced ④ superlative

____ 9. To be an excellent English teacher, what quality do you suppose is required most?
① a systematic understanding of linguistics and pedagogy ② proficiency in English ③ motivating techniques and know-how to maintain interest ④ care and understanding toward learners ⑤ hard work and research for good teaching

____ 10. What is the reason you became or must become an English teacher?
① perceived social status of teaching ② stable salary ③ enough leisure time such as vacations ④ pleasurable school life with students ⑤ others (   )

II. Educational Philosophy and View of Ideal Teacher

____ 1. I believe that the traditional idea of king-teacher-father trinity should still hold good.

____ 2. The relationship between a teacher and learners is essentially that of collaboration in the sense that they are partners.

____ 3. Desirable human behavior is not the product of contingency but of design; therefore, training is important.

____ 4. Teachers are not the main character of class but a mere assistant; it is quite natural that students should select the appropriate programs and be made responsible for their attainment of goals.

____ 5. As a teacher I'm much concerned with self, love, being, spontaneity, creativity, game, humor, naturalness, friendliness, etc.

____ 6. An English teacher is the cultural mediator who is apt to bridge the gap between traditional and western culture.

____ 7. An English teacher should be aware of the ideal of Korean education that children should grow into a hongik-ingan [beneficent human] who will contribute to the establishment of a democratic society.

____ 8. As the society changes, the role of an English teacher ought to be changed as well.

____ 9. There is a big gap as yet between what I am and what I want to be as a teacher.

____ 10. English classrooms have to cover such controversial current issues as war, drug abuse, capital punishment, and environmental protection to increase the awareness of these matters.

____ 11. What do you think is the most important quality that an English teacher should have?

① integrity as an educator ② erudite knowledge of English ③ teaching techniques in the classroom ④ enthusiasm for and commitment to teaching ⑤ others (   )

____ 12. Which of the following is the image of an ideal teacher for the improvement of Korean ELT?
① an austere scholar-like educator ② a charismatic teacher armed with historical awareness ③ a culture-developing teacher focusing on holistic development ④ a democratic teacher who values learner autonomy ⑤ others (   )

III. Classroom Behavior

____ 1. I believe that I give considerable opportunity to students in and outside of the classroom.
____ 2. I usually teach students in consideration of their individual difference.
____ 3. I usually get a lot of feedback from students including questions, complaints and appreciations.
____ 4. I have taught English using TPR (Total Physical Response).
____ 5. I have taught English using a game.
____ 6. I have taught English utilizing the Internet.
____ 7. I have taught English using a computer courseware.
____ 8. In learning English, acquiring an automatic linguistic habit through repetition drills is important.
____ 9. Teachers should intercept the delinquency of a student in order to keep the concentration intact.
____ 10. I can apply whatever method it is, be it individualized teaching, small-group activity, big-group activity, or

multimedia lesson.

____ 11. What would be the most urgent need of yours in making efforts to be a better English teacher?
① Improving English proficiency ② acquisition of pedagogical theories and development of teaching skills ③ Reducing the generation gap to form homogeneity with learners ④ participating in intensive language course abroad and experiencing culture ⑤ others (   )

____ 12. Which is the least proficient area of yours?
① speaking ② listening ③ reading ④ writing

____ 13. What type of teacher do you suppose you are?
① a diligent worker ② a power-wielder ③ a service-provider catering to learners ④ a creative problem-solver ⑤ others (   )

IV. Reflective Self-development

____ 1. Do you often reflect as a teacher on what you have taught how in the classroom?

____ 2. I have written a reflective journal after class or a certain period of time after classroom teaching.

____ 3. I have read an article written by a senior teacher or my peer which gives a vivid depiction of the classroom he or she was in or the lesson taught.

____ 4. I frequently utilize the Internet, visiting the web sites to find out the trend of other teachers and download the materials on line.

____ 5. I have talked about my teaching style with other teachers.

____ 6. I believe that critical reflection on my teaching behav-

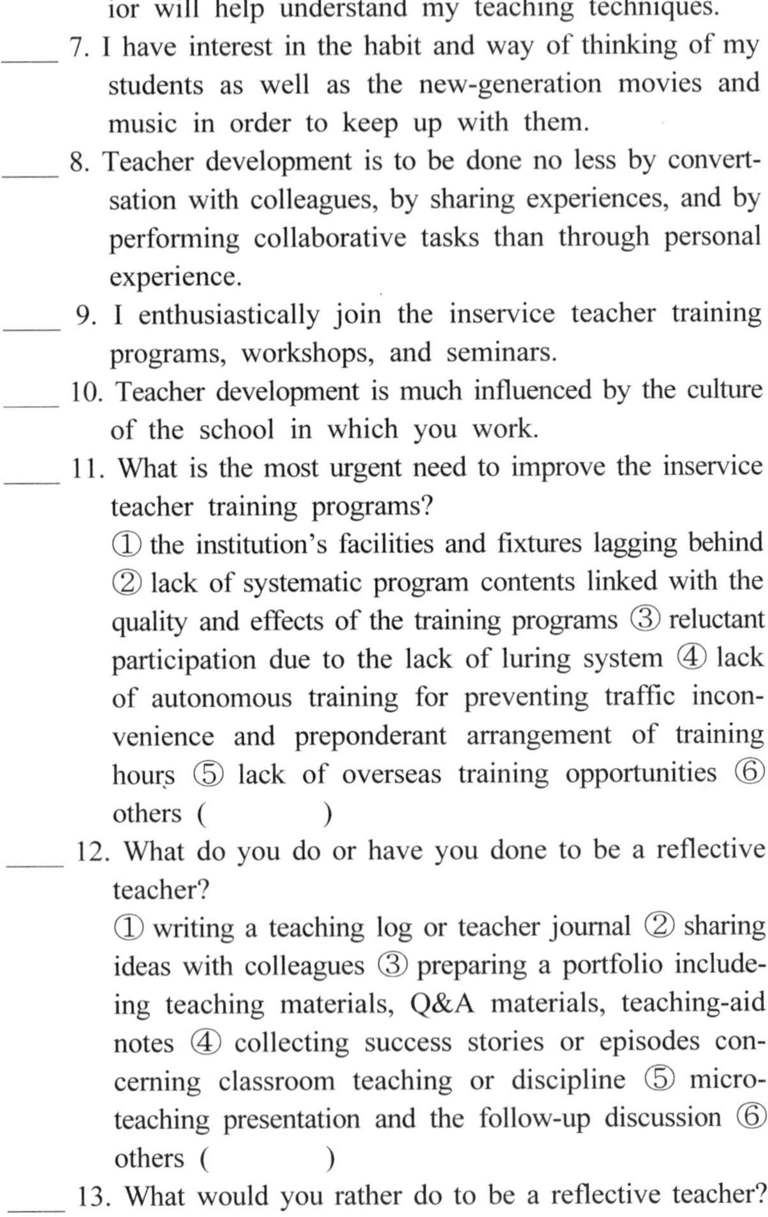

ior will help understand my teaching techniques.

____ 7. I have interest in the habit and way of thinking of my students as well as the new-generation movies and music in order to keep up with them.

____ 8. Teacher development is to be done no less by convertsation with colleagues, by sharing experiences, and by performing collaborative tasks than through personal experience.

____ 9. I enthusiastically join the inservice teacher training programs, workshops, and seminars.

____ 10. Teacher development is much influenced by the culture of the school in which you work.

____ 11. What is the most urgent need to improve the inservice teacher training programs?
① the institution's facilities and fixtures lagging behind ② lack of systematic program contents linked with the quality and effects of the training programs ③ reluctant participation due to the lack of luring system ④ lack of autonomous training for preventing traffic inconvenience and preponderant arrangement of training hours ⑤ lack of overseas training opportunities ⑥ others (   )

____ 12. What do you do or have you done to be a reflective teacher?
① writing a teaching log or teacher journal ② sharing ideas with colleagues ③ preparing a portfolio includeing teaching materials, Q&A materials, teaching-aid notes ④ collecting success stories or episodes concerning classroom teaching or discipline ⑤ microteaching presentation and the follow-up discussion ⑥ others (   )

____ 13. What would you rather do to be a reflective teacher?

① writing a teaching log or teacher journal ② sharing ideas with colleagues ③ preparing a portfolio including teaching materials, Q&A materials, teaching-aid notes ④ collecting success stories or episodes concerning classroom teaching or discipline ⑤ micro-teaching presentation and the follow-up discussion ⑥ others (   )

For the last favor, I would greatly appreciate it if you please answer the following questions about yourself and give your opinion in the space below if you have any questions or something to add regarding the content of the questionnaire. Thank you very much.

Gender: Male ___ Female ___
Age: _____
Teaching Experience: _____ years
Name of Your School: ______________________
E-mail Address: ___________________________
Mailing Address: __________________________

<Opinion>

References

Abrams, M. H. et al. (Eds.) (1962). *The Norton anthology of English literature*. New York: W. W. Norton & Company.

Adamson, B., & Morris, P. (1997). Focus on curriculum change in China and Hong Kong: The English curriculum in the People's Republic of China. *Comparative Education Review*, 41(1): 3-26.

Ahn, H. S. (2000). Naiga gyosayigirul pogihan iyu [The reason I gave up teaching]. *Cheoumchereom*, 18: 36-46.

An, D.-H., & Kang, H.-D. (1997). A teaching model for developing communicative competence based on the Whole Language Approach. *English Teaching*, 52(2): 215-239.

Archambault, R. D. (Ed.) (1964). *John Dewey on education*. Chicago: The University of Chicago Press.

Arita, K. (1989). *Meijin e no Michi—Shakaika Kyoshi*. Tokyo: Nihon Shoseki Kabushikigaisha. Korean translation. *Kyosanun Eotteoke Dallyeondoinunga* [How teachers are tempered]. Lee, K. G. (Trans.) (2001). Seoul: Urikyoyuk.

Bell, B., & Gilbert, J. (1996). *Teacher development: a model from science education*. London: Falmer Press.

Ben-Peretz, M. (2001). The impossible role of teacher educators in a changing world. *Journal of Teacher Education*, 52(1): 48-56.

Bolin, F. S. (1989). Helping student teachers think about teaching: Another look at Lou. *Journal of Teacher Education*, 41(1): 10-19.

Borg, M. (2001). Teachers' beliefs. *ELT Journal*, 55(2): 186-187.

Borko, H., Michalec, P., Timmons, M., & Siddle, J. (1997). Student teaching portfolios: A tool for promoting reflective practice. *Journal of Teacher Education*, 48(5): 345-357.

Brown, H. D. (2000). *Principles of language learning and teaching*. Fourth edition. Longman.

Brown, K. (2001). World Englishes in TESOL programs: An infusion model of curricular innovation. In Hall, D. R., & Hewings, A. (Eds.) (2001). *Innovation in English language teaching: A reader*. London: Routledge. pp. 108-117.

Brumfit, C., Moon, J., & Tongue, R. (Eds.) (1995). *Teaching English to children: From practice to principle*. Longman.

Bruner, J. (1983). *Child's talk: Learning to use language*. New York: Norton.

Buckley, A. (2000). Multicultural reflection. *Journal of Teacher Education*, 51(2): 143-148.

Bullough, R. V. (1989). Teacher education and teacher reflectivity. *Journal of Teacher Education*, 41: 15-21.

Cahn, S. M. (1970). *The philosophical foundations of education*. New York: Harper & Row.

Campbell, D. M., Cignetti, P. B., Melenyzer, B. J., Nettles, D. H., & Wyman, R. M. (2001). *How to develop a professional portfolio: A manual for teachers. Second edition*. Boston: Allyn and Bacon.

Candlin, C. N., & Mercer, N. (Eds.) (2001). *English language teaching in its social context*: A reader. London: Routledge.

Carroll, J. A., Potthoff, D., & Huber, T. (1996). Learning from three years of portfolio use in teacher education. *Journal of Teacher Education*, 47(4): 253-262.

Celce-Murcia, M. (Ed.) (1991). *Teaching English as a second or foreign language*. Second edition. Boston: Heinle & Heinle Publishers.

Choi, S. (2000). Teachers' beliefs about communicative language teaching and their classroom teaching practices. *English Teaching*, 55(4): 3-32.

Chung, Y.-S. (1998). A study on the reality and the ideal of schooling. *Philosophy of Education*, 20: 1-17.

Clemente, A. (2001). The unbearable lightness of EFL. *ELT Journal*, 55(4): 397-402.

Cochran-Smith, M. (2000). In anticipation of our editorship. *Journal of Teacher Education*, 51(2): 85-86.

Confucius, *Da Xue* [The Great Learning]. Retrieved on January 5th, 2002 from the World Wide Web: http://www.sacred-texts.com.

Croft, K. (1980). *Readings on English as a second language*: For teachers and teacher trainees. Boston: Little, Brown and Company.

Cruickshank, D. (1985). *Models for the preparation of America's teachers*. Bloomington, Indiana: Phi Delta Kappa Educational Foundation.

Culler, J. (1983). *On deconstruction: Theory and criticism after struc-*

turalism. London: Routledge & Kegan Paul.

Dakin, M. E. (2001). The poet, the CEO, and the first-grade teacher. *Harvard Educational Review*, 71(2): 269-284.

Dean, J. (1991). *Professional development in school*. Milton Keynes: Open University Press.

Development Committee of the 7th Curriculum for English (1997). *Research on developing the 7th curriculum for English*.

Dewey, J. (1916). *Democracy and education*. New York: The Macmillan Company.

Dewey, J. (1933). *How we think*. Lexington: D. C. Heath and Company.

Eggen, P., & Kauchak, D. (2001). *Educational psychology: Windows on classrooms*. Fifth edition Upper Saddle River, New Jersey: Merrill Prentice Hall.

Ellwein, M. C., & Graue, M. E., & Comfort, R. E. (1989). Talking about instruction: Student teachers' reflections on success and failure in the classroom. *Journal of Teacher Education*, 41(4): 3-14.

Emery, W. G. (1996). Teachers' critical reflection through expert talk. *Journal of Teacher Education*, 47(2): 110-119.

Ethell, R. G., & McMeniman, M. M. (2000). Unlocking the knowledge in action of an expert practitioner. *Journal of Teacher Education*, 51(2): 87-101.

Farrell, T. (2001). Critical friendships: Colleagues helping each other develop. *ELT Journal*, 55(4): 368-374.

Feeney, S., Christensen, D., & Moravcik, E. (2001). *Who am I in the lives of children?: An introduction to teaching young children*. Sixth edition. Upper Saddle River, New Jersey: Merrill Prentice Hall.

Ferguson, P. (1989). A reflective approach to the methods practicum. *Journal of Teacher Education*, 41: 36-41.

Finocchiaro, M., & Brumfit, C. (1983). *The functional-notional approach*. Oxford University Press.

Freiberg, H. J., & Driscoll, A. (2000). *Universal teaching strategies*. Third edition. Boston: Allyn and Bacon.

Fueyo, V., & Koorland, M. A. (1997). Teacher as researcher: A synonym for professionalism. *Journal of Teacher Education*, 48(5): 336-344.

Gabel, S. L. (2001). "I wish my face with dirty water": Narratives of disability and pedagogy. *Journal of Teacher Education*, 52(1):

31-47.

Gorrell, J., & Capron, E. (1989). Cognitive modeling and self-efficacy: Effects on preservice teachers' learning of teaching strategies. *Journal of Teacher Education*, 41(4): 15-22.

Gorsuch, G. J. (2000). EFL educational policies and educational cultures: Influences on teachers' approval of communicative activities. *TESOL Quarterly*, 34(4): 675-710.

Green, A. (2000). Converging paths or ships passing in the night? An 'English' critique of Japanese school reform. *Comparative Education*, 36(4): 417-435.

Hackett, S. C. (1979). *Oriental philosophy: A Westerner's guide to Eastern thought*. The University of Wisconsin Press.

Hall, D. R., & Hewings, A. (Eds.) (2001). *Innovation in English language teaching: A reader*. London: Routledge.

Hamberger, N. M., & Moore, R. L. (1997). From personal to professional values: Conversations about conflicts. *Journal of Teacher Education*, 48(4): 301-310.

Handy, C. (1994). *The age of paradox*. Boston: Harvard Business School Press.

Hatton, N., & Smith, D. (1995). Reflection in teacher education: Towards definition and implementation. *Teaching & Teacher Education*, 11(1): 33-49.

Healey, J. F. (1993). *Statistics: A tool for social research*. Third edition. Belmont, California: Wadsworth Publishing Company.

Henderson, J. G. (1989). Positioned reflective practice: A curriculum discussion. *Journal of Teacher Education*, 41: 10-14.

Hill, L. (2000). What does it take to change minds? Intellectual development of preservice teachers. *Journal of Teacher Education*, 51(1): 50-62.

Hollingsworth, S. (Ed.) (1997). *International action research: A casebook for educational reform*. London: Falmer Press.

Hornsey, A. (1994). Authenticity in foreign language learning. In Roberts, T. (Ed.). *Languages Forum* 2(3): 6-7. London: Institute of Education.

Howatt, A. P. R. (1984). A *history of English language teaching*. Oxford University Press.

Huggett, A. J., & Stinnett, T. M. (1956). *Professional Problems of*

Teachers. New York: The Macmillan Company.

Huh, B. G. (1994). Kyojik seonggyeok gochal: Kyojikeui jeonmunjikseonge gwanhan banseongjeok noneui [Considering the Characteristics of Teaching: A Retrospective Discussion on the Professionality of Teaching]. *Pedagogical Studies*, 32(1): 49-78.

Jackson, D. O. (2001). Language-related episodes. *ELT Journal*, 55(3): 298-299.

Jennings, Z. (2001). Teacher education in selected countries in the Commonwealth Caribbean: The ideal of policy versus the reality of practice. *Comparative Education*, 37(1): 107-134.

Jeon, J.-H., & Kim, E.-J. (2001). Teacher training through self-observation. *Applied Linguistics*, (17)2: 157-177.

Jeong, I. H. (1999). Kyowonui jeonmunjeok nungnyeok jego bangan [Ways to enhance the professional competency of teachers]. *Yeonsunonchong*, 17: 81-99.

Joe, J.-O., & Matheson, G. (1996). Two participants in a teacher development group report back. *Duksungyeodainonmunjip*, 25: 91-104.

Joyce, B., & Weil, M. (1996). *Models of teaching*. Fifth edition. Boston: Allyn and Bacon.

Jung, J.-A. (2001). *An analysis of teacher candidates' and English teachers' view on English teacher training*. MA thesis.

Jung, Y. S. (2001). Toward an effective EFL teacher development program focusing on multimedia and the Internet. *English Teaching*, 56(4): 141-162.

Kagan, D. M. (1992). Professional growth among preservice and beginning teachers. *Review of Educational Research*, 62(2): 129-169.

Kahne, J., & Westheimer, J. (2000). A pedagogy of collective action and reflection. *Journal of Teacher Education*, 51(5): 372-383.

Kamhi-Stein, L. D. (2000). Looking to the future of TESOL teacher education: Web-based bulletin board discussions in a methods course. *TESOL Quarterly*, 34(3): 423-455.

Kang, Y. O. (2001). *A study on the self-training realities of secondary school English teachers in Ulsan*. MA thesis.

Kasper, G., & Kellerman, E. (Eds.): (1997). *Communication strategies: Psycholinguistic and sociolinguistic perspectives*. London: Longman.

Killen, L. R. (1989). Reflecting on reflective teaching: A response. *Journal of Teacher Education*, 41: 49-52.

Kim, B.-S. (2001). *The effect of teacher belief system on English instruction*. MA Thesis.

Kim, D.-K. (2001). CLT and TETE for non-native teachers: A reading comprehension approach. *Applied Linguistics*, (17)2: 55-72.

Kim, J.-W. (2000). Methodological changes in TEFL research in Korea and new directions for the future. *English Teaching*, 55(4): 345-366.

Kim, Y. J. (1999). Kyojik jeongcheseongui tamgurul wihan bunseokjeok yeongu [An analytical research in search for teachers' professional identity]. *Teacher Education*, 16(2): 49-79.

Kim, C.-H. (1998). An agenda for change in English education in Korea. *The Journal of English Language Teaching*, 9: 189-206.

Kolb, D. (1984). *Experiential Learning*. Englewood Cliffs, New Jersey: Prentice-Hall.

Korea Educational Development Institute (1997). *The 7th English curriculum development research*. Seoul: Korea Educational Development Institute.

Korea General Association of Teacher Organization (1998). Kyowon-jeongchaik hyeonane daihan kyowon insik josa yeongu [A survey research on teachers' perceptions of current agenda for teacher policies]. Seoul: Korea General Association of Teacher Organization.

Kramsch, C. (1993). *Context and culture in language teaching*. Oxford: Westview Press.

Krashen, S. D., & Terrell, T. D. (1983). *The natural approach: Language acquisition in the classroom*. Oxford: Pergamon Press.

Krouse, S. (1996). Portfolios in teacher education: Effects of instruction on preservice teachers' early comprehension of the portfolio process. *Journal of Teacher Education*, 47(2): 130-138.

Labaree, D. F. (1992). Power, knowledge, and the rationalization of teaching: A genealogy of the movement to professionalize teaching. *Harvard Educational Review*, 62(2): 123-154.

Labaree, D. F. (2000). On the nature of teaching and teacher education: Difficult practices that look easy. *Journal of Teacher Education*, 51(3): 228-233.

Lee, D. H. (2000). 21segiui kyosasanggwa kyojik [The image of a teacher in the 21st century and the profession of teaching]. *Korea Teacher Education*, 17(1): 1-18.

Lee, W., Choi, Y. H., Boo, K.-S., & Lee, J.-W. (2001). An investigation into the effects of elementary English education: A follow-up study on first-year middle school students. *English Teaching*, 56(4): 211-241.

Li, D. (1998). "It's always more difficult than you plan and imagine": Teachers' perceived difficulties in introducing the communicative approach in South Korea. *TESOL Quarterly*, 32(4): 677-703.

Lieberman, A. (2000). Networks as learning communities: Shaping the future of teacher development. *Journal of Teacher Education*, 51(3): 221-227.

Lightbown, P. M. & Spada, N. (2006). *How languages are learned*. New York: Oxford University Press.

Lortie, D. C. (1975). *Schoolteacher: A sociological study*. Chicago: University of Chicago.

MacIntyre, P. D., & Gardner, R. C. (1988). Anxiety and second-language learning: Toward a theoretical clarification. *Language Learning*, 39(2): 251-275.

Mahlios, M., & Maxson, M. (1995). Capturing preservice teachers' beliefs about schooling, life, and childhood. *Journal of Teacher Education*, 46(3): 192-199.

Maxwell, R. J., & Meiser, M. J. (2001). *Teaching English in middle and secondary schools*. Third edition. Upper Saddle River, New Jersey: Merrill Prentice Hall.

McDermott, P., Gormley, K., Rothenberg, J., & Hammer, J. (1995). The influence of classroom practica experiences on student teachers' thoughts about teaching. *Journal of Teacher Education*, 46(3): 184-191.

McDonough, J., & Shaw, C. (1993). *Materials and methods in ELT*: A teacher's guide. Oxford: Blackwell.

Meyen, E. L. (1972). *Developing units of instruction: For the mentally retarded and other children with learning problems*. Dubuque, Iowa: Wm. C. Brown Company Publishers.

Milton, J. S., McTeer, P. M., & Corbet, J. J. (1997). Introduction to statistics. New York: The McGraw-Hill Companies, Inc.

Mohan, B., Leung, C., & Davison, C. (Eds.) (2001). *English as a second language in the mainstream: Teaching, learning and identity.* Singapore: Pearson Education.

Mok, Y. H. (1995). *Hu Hyeondaijuui Gyoyukhak* [Postmodernism education]. Seoul: Gyoyukgwahaksa.

Moore, G. W. (1983). *Developing and evaluating educational research.* Boston: Little, Brown and Company.

Namoto, M., Kinoshita, M., Takubo, C., Kiyonaga, K., Kawajiri, M., & Kanamori, T. (2000). Present Situation of English Education in Japan. *The Journal of English Language Teaching*, 12(1): 1-29.

Newmann, F. & Wehlage, G. (1995). *Successful school restructuring.* Madison: Center on Organization and Restructuring of Schools, University of Wisconsin-Madison.

Norton, B. (1997). Language, identity, and the ownership of English. *TESOL Quarterly*, 31(3): 409-429.

Nunan, D. (1999). *Second language teaching & learning.* Boston: Heinle & Heinle Publishers.

O'Donoghue, T. A., & Brooker, R. (1996). The rhetoric and the reality of the promotion of reflection during practice teaching: An Australian case study. *Journal of Teacher Education*, 47(2): 99-109.

Okano, K., & Tsuchiya, M. (1999). *Education in contemporary Japan: Inequality and diversity.* Cambridge University Press.

Oller, J. W. (Ed.) (1993). *Methods that work.* Boston: Heinle & Heinle Publishers.

Orlich, D. C., Harder, R. J., Callahan, R. C., & Gibson, H. W. (1998). *Teaching strategies: A guide to better instruction.* Fifth edition. Boston: Houghton Mifflin Company.

Oxford, R. (Ed.) (1996). *Language learning strategies around the world: Cross-cultural perspectives.* University of Hawai'i: Second Language Teaching & Curriculum Center.

Pachler, N., & Field, K. (1997). *Learning to teach modern foreign languages in the secondary school: A companion to school experience.* London: Routledge.

Pae, D.-B. (2000). The development of teacher education program models for English teachers in elementary and secondary schools. *The Journal of English Language Teaching*, 12(1): 113-144.

Park, K. S. (1987). *Developing a communicative language teaching model for junior highschool EFL sophomores in Korea based on text-book/learner-needs analysis*. MA thesis.

Paulston, C. B., & Bruder, M. N. (1976). *Teaching English as a second language: Techniques and procedures*. Boston: Little, Brown and Company.

Pratte, R., & Rury, J. L. (1991). Teachers, professionalism, and craft. *Teachers College Record*, 93(1): 125-138.

Preskill, S. L., & Jacobvitz, R. S. (2001). *Stories of teaching: A foundation for educational renewal*. Upper Saddle River, New Jersey: Merrill Prentice Hall.

Richard-amato, P. A. (2003). *Making it happen: From interactive to participatory language teaching*. Third Edition. London: Pearson-Longman.

Richards, J. C., & Lockhart, C. (1994). *Reflective teaching in second language classrooms*. Cambridge University Press.

Richert, A. E. (1990). Teaching teachers to reflect: A consideration of programme structure. *Journal of Curriculum Studies*, 22: 507-509.

Rhine, S. (1995). The challenge of effectively preparing teachers of Limited-English-Proficient students. *Journal of Teacher Education*, 46(3): 381-389.

Roberts, J. (1998). *Language teacher education*. London: Arnold.

Ross, D. D. (1989). First steps in developing a reflective approach. *Journal of Teacher Education*, 41: 22-30.

Roth, R. A. (1989). Preparing the reflective practitioner: Transforming the apprentice through the dialectic. *Journal of Teacher Education*, 41: 31-35.

Schön, D. A. (1983). *The reflective practitioner: How professionals think in action*. New York: Basic Books, Inc.

Schön, D. A. (1987). *Educating the reflective practitioner*. San Francisco: Jossey-Bass.

Seliger, H. W., & Shohamy E. (1989). *Second language research methods*. Oxford: Oxford University Press.

Shin, G. (2001). English language teaching system change to enhance the social justice and the efficiency of the national economy. *English Teaching*, 56(2): 193-218.

Shulman, L. S. (1987). Knowledge and teaching: Foundations of the new reform. *Harvard Educational Review*, 57(1): 1-22.

Smith, J. (2001). Modeling the social construction of knowledge in ELT teacher education. *ELT Journal*, 55(3): 221-227.

Smyth, J. (1989). Developing and sustaining critical reflection in teacher education. *Journal of Teacher Education*, 41: 2-9.

Smyth, J. (1992). Teachers' work and the politics of reflection. *American Educational Research Journal*, 29(2): 267-300.

Song, M. J. (1997). Teaching effective communication strategies to Korean learners of English. *English Teaching*, 52(2): 75-93.

Sparks-Langer, G. M., Simmons, J. M., Pasch, M., Colton, A., & Starko, A. (1989). Reflective pedagogical thinking: How can we promote it and measure it? *Journal of Teacher Education*, 41(4): 23-32.

Thornbury, S. (2001). The unbearable lightness of EFL. *ELT Journal*, 55(4): 391-396.

Titone, R. (1968). *Teaching foreign languages: An historical sketch.* Washington, D.C.: Georgetown University Press.

Tom, A. R. (1985). Inquiring into inquiry-oriented teacher education. *Journal of Teacher Education*, 36(5): 35-44.

Tom, A. R. (1997). *Redesigning teacher education.* State University of New York Press.

Tomlinson, B. (Ed.) (1998). *Materials development in language teaching.* Cambridge University Press.

Tremmel, R. (1993). Zen and the art of reflective practice in teacher education. *Harvard Educational Review*, 63: 434-458.

UNESCO (1970). *Practical guide to inservice teacher training in Africa: Establishment, execution and control of training programmes.*

Van Lier, L. (1988). *The classroom and the language teacher: Ethnography and second-language classroom research.* London: Longman.

Van Lier, L. (1996). *Interaction in the language curriculum: Awareness, autonomy and authenticity.* London: Longman.

Van Manen, J. (1977). Linking ways of knowing with ways of being practical. *Curriculum Inquiry*, 6: 205-208.

Wallace, M. J. (1991). *Training foreign language teachers: A reflective approach.* Cambridge University Press.

Weinstein, C. S. (1989). Teacher education students' preconceptions of teaching. *Journal of Teacher Education*, 41: 53-60.

Weldon, L. L. (1971). *Conflicts in our schools.* Columbus, Ohio: Charles E. Merrill Publishing Company.

White, R. V. (1988). *The ELT curriculum: Design, innovation and management*. Blackwell Publishers.

Widdowson, H. G. (1990). *Aspects of Language Teaching*. Oxford: Oxford University Press.

Willis, D. (2003). *Rules, patterns and words: grammar and lexis in English language teaching*. Cambridge: Cambridge University Press.

Wilson, J. (1986). The teaching profession: a case of self-mutilation. *Journal of Philosophy of Education*, 20(2): 245-250.

Wu, Y. (2001). English language teaching in China: Trends and challenges. *TESOL Quarterly*, 35(1): 191-198.

Yost, D. S., Sentner, S. M., & Forlenza-Bailey, A. (2000). An examination of the construct of critical reflection: Implications for teacher education programming in the 21st century. *Journal of Teacher Education*, 51(1): 39-49.

Zeichner, K. M., & Liston, D. P. (1987). Teaching student teachers to reflect. *Harvard Educational Review*, 57(1): 23-48.

Index

D

E

F

G

H

I

J

K

L

M

N

O

P

Q

R

S

T

U

V

W

Z

저자 소개: 박길수(朴桔洙)

저자는 미국 University of Kansas 대학원을 졸업했고
중앙대학교에서 영어교육학 박사학위를 받았으며
육군3사관학교와 안양대학교 교수를 역임하였다.
현재 중앙대학교 영어교육과에 출강하면서
저술가와 출판기획 전문가로 활동하고 있다.
저서: 『내일의 크리스천 지도자를 위한 영어』(어학마을, 2004)
『우리는 영어를 어떻게 배우는가』(지문당, 2008)
역서: 『증권분석』(벤저민 그레이엄 저, 리딩리더, 2008)

한국에서의 성찰 언어교육 값 18,000원

2009년 2월 20일 1판 1쇄

저 자	박 길 수
발 행 인	임 삼 규
발 행 처	**지 문 당**
주 소	413-756 경기도 파주시 교하읍 문발리 514-7(본사) 110-360 서울시 종로구 와룡동 95번지(서울사무소)
등 록	1997. 12. 30. 제1-2268호
영 업 부	(02)743-3192~3 팩스(02)742-4657
전자우편	sale@jimoon.co.kr
편 집 부	(02)743-0227 팩스(02)743-3097
전자우편	edit@jimoon.co.kr
홈페이지	www.jimoon.co.kr

ISBN 978-89-6297-006-7